CW00970744

Profile Pentagram Design

Edited by Susan Yelavich

CONTENTS

The Culture(s) of Pentagram

by Susan Yelavich

Above: The international partners' meeting,
New York, November 2003.

PENTAGRAM HAS ALWAYS TAKEN CARE to carve its name into the woodwork of design ('s nascent) history. Its partners have produced no less than six publications about the firm since its inception in 1972—roughly one every five years. However, this book is a departure. Instead of a singular self-portrait, it offers a gallery of profiles. Hence, the parenthetical, verging-on-heretical *s* in the title of this essay.

As much as *Profile* may be read as nineteen egos gone wild, the book represents an evolution in the particular persona that is Pentagram. By embracing the premise of the serial portrait over a singular silhouette, Pentagram is once again stretching, flexing its considerable design muscle, getting ready for its next sprint into the new millennium. There is a recognition that clients and colleagues, as well as mentees, students, and historians of design, will benefit enormously from a sharper understanding of the commonalities that bind and the idiosyncrasies that inflect the character of Pentagram.

It is true that Pentagram's very existence is predicated on the idea of collaborative interdisciplinary practice, with an all-for-one-and-one-for-all esprit de corps. That hasn't changed. But as the firm has evolved, it is also true that, depending on which side of the Atlantic or, for that matter, which coast of the States one views them from, Pentagram looks and feels subtly different. Moreover, as in any family that perpetuates its lines of succession so carefully, there are distinct generational characteristics that enrich the gene pool: the quiet middle children promoted (versus recruited) to partnership, the young Turks eager to insinuate new ideas, and the steadfast minders of the shop.

Staying with the metaphor of choice, we may come to understand Pentagram a bit better if we think of its nature as comprising dominant and recessive qualities. If you ask the insiders—the partners—they'll say that the dominant conviction is that Pentagram is about ideas. Looking in from the outside, what seems most dominant is that Pentagram is held together by respect for one anothers' ideas, however you interpret the word "idea," be it a pithy, succinct solution, a strategy for achieving it, or the formal invention it has spawned. Pentagram operates on a system of mutual respect (and affection) that isn't burdened with the entanglements of love. In the parlance of design, it works precisely because there is no strong party line on aesthetics. Content is king. Pentagram's most senior partner, John McConnell, observes, "We may be 'polemic averse,' but we are idea rich." A sentiment refracted back by one of the newest partners, Abbott Miller: "You can only add to the mixture; you can't shape it or censor it. That's the problem of democracy." And, it goes without saying, its virtue.

<hr>

Opposite: Pentagram's London office.

Pentagram may have an allergy to theory, but it is steeped in a utopian ideal, albeit a decidedly capitalist utopia of catholic tastes. As Colin Forbes, one of the founding fathers, declaimed in his Pentagram constitution, "The idea of equality goes back to our first company, Fletcher/Forbes/Gill, where the three partners decided on equal equity and equal incomes. However, each partner's profitability was openly declared, which contributed to a competitive element."[1]

Equality is the operative idea: All partners practice, maintaining their own studios and staff. As John Rushworth says, they all "keep their hands dirty." All partners share in the tasks of running the show—whether it's squaring accounts or producing a product—like this one. And it is in this respect, in the rotating of "corporate" responsibilities, that one gets a sense of communal roots deeper than Forbes's economics. A sense of the social, even socialist, ethos that marked the late '60s and early '70s—the climate in which Pentagram germinated.

Pentagram became the grown-up ideal of the commune that every college student since the '60s has fantasized would save them from the alienation of soul-stripping work. Grown-up because they admit and court the realpolitik of commerce; ideal because they truly believe in design's potency

to modulate the alienating aspects of commerce, shunned not just in the free-love era but also back in the day of their bohemian Bauhaus grandparents. (Indeed, there's a doctoral thesis waiting to be written about the Pentagram's place in the history of craft-based utopian communities.)

Pentagram operates in contrast to those agents of change who deploy extreme tactics, those necessary social catalysts who, in their urgency, thrive on the fringe and work in the margins. Like every community, design has its share of provocateurs, whether testing limits with hermetic work or legitimately breaking new ground. They are the kind of people who are comfortable being uncomfortable. Pentagram is plainly, even proudly, not. Pentagram's partners are constitutionally too congenial, collegial, and, philosophically, too patient. (Michael Bierut claims he suffers from a "crippling politeness." His riposte to manifesto is footnoted reason.[2]) Suspicious of the ephemeral nature of style, Pentagram partners prefer to take the long view and see the world through a wide-angle lens. Tiny projects for small groups of people don't hold their interest. Too much work for too little impact—and no doubt, too little compensation (unless it's pro bono work, estimated to represent a significant 10 to 15 percent of Pentagram's practice).

However, Pentagram's commitment to projects of scale has a social dimension of its own. Virtually

Opposite: Pentagram's New York office.

all of the partners are committed populists who, not coincidentally, hail from middle- and working-class backgrounds themselves. Implicit in their worldview: Life should be better for everyone, and everyone should be included in the conversation.

There is a tacit acceptance of the modernist agenda of well-being through design. It is evident in the formal qualities of much of the work. Even so, faith in the ameliorating aspect of design is a matter of degree. Tactically, some partners feel that Pentagram's best way of affecting culture at large is within the confines of client-driven projects. Others, without discounting that possibility, would like to transcend traditional practice. The appeal of civic works, of their possibilities in the next phase of Pentagram's maturity, seems particularly American. Kit Hinrichs would like to figure out a way to tackle the shoddy, tilt-up architecture of cheesy hotels surrounding US airports. Lisa Strausfeld would like to make the figures of campaign finance more graphic, more transparent; she'd like to see better data sets on cancer and the environment.

Perhaps not surprisingly, there is a more international caste of concerns on the other side of the Atlantic. Rushworth wonders about "the extent to which Pentagram can counter global conformity." The challenge being that many of their clients contribute to that numbing matrix.

They may have found part of the solution in their own culture. The predominantly Anglo-Saxon London office has become increasingly heterogeneous with relatively recent additions of Lorenzo Apicella, Fernando Gutiérrez, and Angus Hyland (though they've yet to hire a female partner). And in June of 2003, Justus Oehler set up Pentagram Berlin, forwarding Pentagram's ambitions to expand its practice and his own interests in negotiating cultural borders.

Another kind of utopian frame of reference that crops up frequently is religion, though it is more common in the US where there's perhaps less reserve about personal revelations. Conversations (and this book's essays) are peppered with ecclesiastical references. Confused former altar boy Bierut cited their "Torah" of criteria for partnership. Jim Biber, the architect, likened Pentagram to a Quaker meetinghouse, where everyone speaks out (and is outspoken). Lowell Williams referred to Pentagram's partners and teams as "pastors and churches in one religion." (Scher is apparently religious only about reading the *New York Times* and the *New Yorker*. With no thoughts to the hereafter, unfazed by existential angst, she lives completely in the present.)

By now the transposition of such metaphors into the realm of visual culture at large is familiar: the museum as temple, the last place of meditation, and

Above: Pentagram's San Francisco office.

so on. That may account in part for the liberal use of religious references, but in the context of Pentagram, the linguistic cues all point to an unusual reverence for the bonds of professional marriage. Divorce is relatively rare. The strength of the relationships at Pentagram is such that the partners are remarkably direct with one another. None of the usual subterfuge endemic to conventional institutional culture is necessary. They're not afraid to "grow by fight," according to Scher. What Williams calls a "well-armored ego" is prerequisite Pentagram gear, and wit, the weapon of choice.

Verbal thrust-and-parry rises to an art in the UK, where the religion is the word. (Colin Forbes famously claimed that, at Pentagram, "an idea isn't an idea unless it can be explained over the phone.") Here, pieties are suspect, and "club" substitutes for "church" in frank self-appraisal. There is an overlay of irony, a "nod and wink," says Angus Hyland of the London office's modus operandi. Rushworth gauges new members in terms of whether they're "clubbable." Fernando talks about the security that comes of inheriting a way of doing things, and yet he is aware of the constant testing that infuses that culture: Competitive humor is inseparable from competitive work. Skillful repartee—getting there first—is considered a mark of intelligence.

Opposite: Pentagram's Austin office

Though when it comes to the work of design, Daniel Weil says, "We don't need to share our thoughts...there's an extracorporeal dimension to Pentagram." (He must sometimes wish that to be literally true, given how often he flies to New York to work with Michael Gericke and other partners.) That comfort with intuitive exchange versus argumentative debate filters into Pentagram UK's public persona as well. It tends to listen more than it pronounces. The London office is host to regular public events. Its Notting Hill gallery and office serve as a venue for exhibitions and lectures, whereas the New York partners, in particular, are regular contributors to professional journals and familiar voices on the lecture circuit. London's Lorenzo Apicella acknowledges a certain reticence about being "overly promotional," noting a residual aversion to selling in the UK. Woody Pirtle, by turn, envies his London partners' exhibition opportunities.

Maintaining relevance within the design community is, of course, a relative affair. David Hillman thinks about it less in peripherals and more in terms of practice, musing that graphic design may not be the mainstay of Pentagram in ten years' time, citing the recent explosion of small consultancies. Charting a trajectory of design, however, has not been the central preoccupation of Pentagram. They are adamant that they progress through the addition of new partners, whether into the realm of technology

Above: Pentagram's Berlin office.

with Bob Brunner or into editorial waters with DJ Stout. Though it may be tempting to read the appointment of digital mediologist Lisa Strausfeld as a calculated act of futurism, at Pentagram, professional chemistry counts for more than crystal-ball analysis. Even Justus Oehler's move to Berlin was his personal choice, not a corporate move to gain better access to Eastern European markets.

Pentagram's continued act of faith in its philosophy of growth through partners (vs. five-year plans) coincides with the current reprise of the larger notion of authorship. In a recent *New York Times Book Review*, Sven Birkerts writes, "Reading...the new book by Harold Bloom celebrating the cult of genius, I wonder if we might not be seeing signs of revolt against the long dominance of 'theory' in the literary arena, an attempt...to return the artist to mythic centrality and to reinvigorate old assumptions about hierarchies of excellence."[3]

Substitute "design" for "literary" and you get the picture. And, if Birkerts is right, this may be Pentagram's next moment. From its beginnings, by virtue of its partner/author structure, Pentagram has been impervious to any unifying "theory." It was built and continues to prosper on tacit understandings. "Ideas," Pentagram's self-professed stock-in-trade, are not theories.

To embroider on McConnell, design today is theory weak but opportunity rich. We've just come through the end of the conflict between the modern and the postmodern, between a stagnating, exclusive monotheism and a promiscuous polytheism, dissolved in irrelevance. As a result, there is a greater interest in the personal, a less constipated view of what it means to be contemporary, to be relevant. Pentagram, by nature, is poised to flourish in this climate. Designers are free to mine history deeply—the postmodern legacy—and constrained to internalize their findings, not just identify them—the modern legacy. Furthermore, out of a growing understanding that design did not spring sui generis from the Industrial Revolution, there has been an explosion of new resources, a deepening of memory. Just how, and through whom, Pentagram chooses to mine the expanding universe of possibilities will ultimately assure the design firm's relevance.

1. Colin Forbes, "Transition," 1992.
2. Bierut responded to *Adbusters*' "First Things First Manifesto" (a document written and signed by graphic designers advocating practicing in service to an explicitly social agenda) point by point in his piece "A Manifesto with Ten Footnotes," published in the March/April 2000 issue of *I.D. Magazine*.
3. Excerpted from Birkerts's review of William Gaddis's last book, *Agapé Agape*: "Parting Shots," *New York Times Book Review*, October 6, 2002. Birkerts's personal opinion is that any reinvigoration of hierarchies of excellence is actually doomed.

The Idea
of Pentagram

by Rick Poynor

WHEN AN ORGANIZATION IS AS LONG-LIVED and well established as Pentagram, it is almost inevitable that at a certain point in its development, people will stop perceiving it clearly for what it is. It becomes, to put it bluntly, part of the scenery, a bump in the landscape rather than a structure understood to be the outcome of dynamic subterranean forces. After more than thirty years in business, Pentagram maintains a well-earned reputation, in Britain and the United States and beyond, for producing graphic design, products, and environments of the highest standard, but the aspect of Pentagram that is arguably most original, indeed unique, is less well understood by observers, especially by those who are unclear about the company's origins and founding principles. Pentagram is, above all, a model of collaborative and independent practice, of shared revenues and pooled talent. The company has found the answer to the dilemma that many designers face in the middle of their careers: How do I sustain my current position; how can I increase the opportunities available to me; and having reached this level, what should I do next?

Virtually every Pentagram partner has come to this juncture by the time they join. Most will have spent at least a decade, sometimes longer, running their own companies. They will be successful at what they do and will have achieved a high level of national and even international acclaim among fellow designers. They will probably have attained many of the goals they set out to attain when they began their careers. Their companies are unlikely to be especially large. These designers will be keenly aware of the tremendous size achieved by globally inclined design groups that prioritize growth, but they will have resolved not to grow too big themselves, understanding that, according to the traditional management model, this will require them to stop designing and become managers. In any case, many designers having midcareer second thoughts will possess little aptitude for business, and this is the most common reason why even the most celebrated designers sometimes end up running aground. What the successful midcareer designer

Opposite: The evolving Pentagram partnership, 1972–2003 (taken from Paula Scher's book Make it Bigger, *Princeton Architectural Press, 2002).*

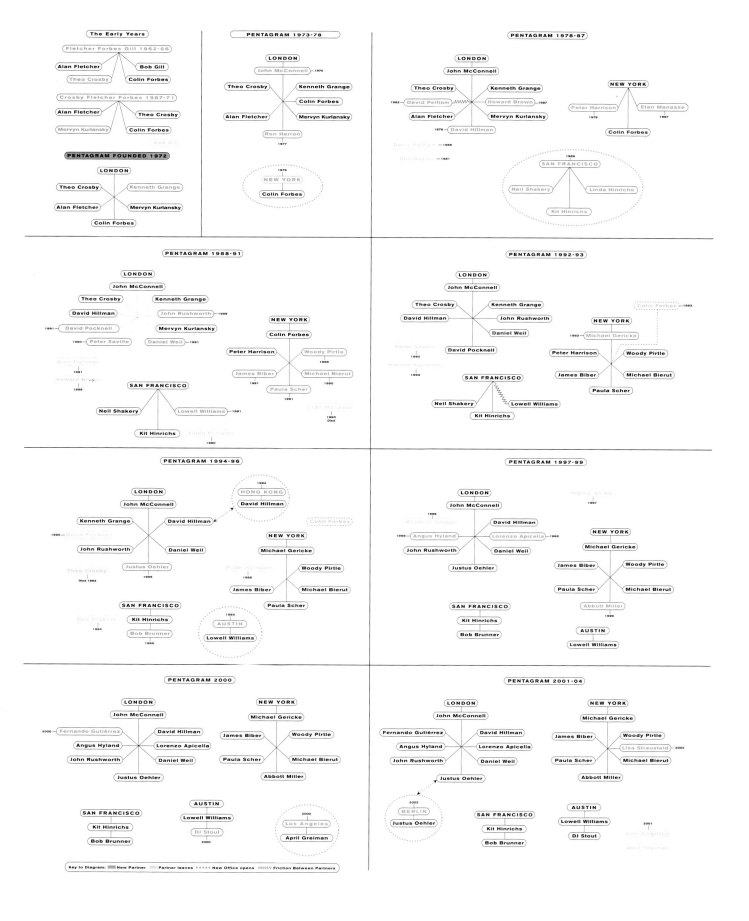

The Early Years

Fletcher Forbes Gill 1962-66
Alan Fletcher
Bob Gill
Theo Crosby
Colin Forbes

Crosby Fletcher Forbes 1967-71
Alan Fletcher
Theo Crosby
Mervyn Kurlansky
Colin Forbes
Bob Gill

PENTAGRAM FOUNDED 1972

LONDON
Theo Crosby
Kenneth Grange
Alan Fletcher
Mervyn Kurlansky
Colin Forbes

PENTAGRAM 1973-78

LONDON
John McConnell — 1974
Theo Crosby
Kenneth Grange
Colin Forbes
Alan Fletcher
Mervyn Kurlansky
Ron Herron
1977

1978
NEW YORK
Colin Forbes

PENTAGRAM 1978-87

LONDON
John McConnell
Theo Crosby
Kenneth Grange
1982 David Pelham ⋙ Howard Brown — 1987
Alan Fletcher
Mervyn Kurlansky
1978 David Hillman
David Pelham — 1986
Nick Harmer — 1981

NEW YORK
Peter Harrison
Etan Manasse
1978
1987
Colin Forbes

1986
SAN FRANCISCO
Neil Shakery
Linda Hinrichs
Kit Hinrichs

PENTAGRAM 1988-91

LONDON
John McConnell
Theo Crosby
Kenneth Grange
David Hillman
John Rushworth — 1989
1991 — David Pocknell
Mervyn Kurlansky
1990 — Peter Saville
Daniel Weil — 1991
Alan Fletcher
1991
Howard Brown
1988

NEW YORK
Colin Forbes
Peter Harrison
Woody Pirtle
1988
James Biber
Michael Bierut
1991
1990
Paula Scher
1991
Etan Manasse
1990
Died

SAN FRANCISCO
Neil Shakery
Lowell Williams — 1991
Kit Hinrichs
Linda Hinrichs
1990

PENTAGRAM 1992-93

LONDON
John McConnell
Theo Crosby
Kenneth Grange
David Hillman
John Rushworth
Daniel Weil
Peter Saville
1992
David Pocknell
Mervyn Kurlansky
1993

Colin Forbes — 1993
NEW YORK
1993 — Michael Gericke
Peter Harrison
Woody Pirtle
James Biber
Michael Bierut
Paula Scher

SAN FRANCISCO
Neil Shakery
Lowell Williams
Kit Hinrichs

PENTAGRAM 1994-96

LONDON
John McConnell
Kenneth Grange
David Hillman
1995 — David Pocknell
John Rushworth
Daniel Weil
Justus Oehler
1995
Theo Crosby
Died 1994

1994
HONG KONG
David Hillman

NEW YORK
Michael Gericke
Woody Pirtle
James Biber
Michael Bierut
Paula Scher
Peter Harrison
1996

Colin Forbes

SAN FRANCISCO
Kit Hinrichs
Bob Brunner
Neil Shakery
1994

1994
AUSTIN
Lowell Williams
1996

PENTAGRAM 1997-99

LONDON
John McConnell
David Hillman
Kenneth Grange
1998
Angus Hyland
Lorenzo Apicella — 1996
John Rushworth
Daniel Weil
Justus Oehler

HONG KONG
1997

NEW YORK
Michael Gericke
James Biber
Woody Pirtle
Paula Scher
Michael Bierut
Abbott Miller
1999

SAN FRANCISCO
Kit Hinrichs
Bob Brunner

AUSTIN
Lowell Williams

PENTAGRAM 2000

LONDON
John McConnell
2000 — Fernando Gutiérrez
David Hillman
Angus Hyland
Lorenzo Apicella
John Rushworth
Daniel Weil
Justus Oehler

NEW YORK
Michael Gericke
James Biber
Woody Pirtle
Paula Scher
Michael Bierut
Abbott Miller

SAN FRANCISCO
Kit Hinrichs
Bob Brunner

AUSTIN
Lowell Williams
DJ Stout
2000

2000
Los Angeles
April Greiman

PENTAGRAM 2001-04

LONDON
John McConnell
Fernando Gutiérrez
David Hillman
Angus Hyland
Lorenzo Apicella
John Rushworth
Daniel Weil
Justus Oehler

2002
BERLIN
Justus Oehler

NEW YORK
Michael Gericke
James Biber
Woody Pirtle
Lisa Strausfeld — 2002
Paula Scher
Michael Bierut
Abbott Miller

SAN FRANCISCO
Kit Hinrichs
Bob Brunner

AUSTIN
Lowell Williams
DJ Stout
2001
Los Angeles
April Greiman

Key to Diagram: ▬ New Partner ▭ Partner leaves ••••• New Office opens ⋙ Friction Between Partners

will almost certainly possess is a generously sized ego, and it is their ability to keep this under control in an environment that the partners freely admit is full of similarly "oversize" egos that will determine whether they can find a viable way to operate within Pentagram's idiosyncratic framework. Assuming, that is, that the partners would like them to join the club in the first place.

Even in their early days as Fletcher/Forbes/Gill and Crosby/Fletcher/Forbes, before they became Pentagram in 1972, the partners saw the company as a means of aggregating their abilities and boosting their capability as a collective, without having to sacrifice their individuality and freedom. Pentagram is guided by essentially the same principle today. Joining as a partner also brings increased exposure and opportunities that are not available to a designer running his or her own small company. Invited to become a partner two years after Pentagram's inception, John McConnell wanted to know what he had to gain from such a move. Once installed, he discovered that the effect on his development as a designer "was like jumping forward 15 years at one stride."[1] Paula Scher, who became a partner in 1991, acknowledges that there is some loss of autonomy—this is why egos must be reined in—but in return, a new partner enjoys greater possibilities. "At Pentagram," writes Scher, "I have attained the power, status and credibility to more easily persuade clients to a given design."[2]

For three decades, Pentagram has sustained a difficult balancing act between commerce and culture. Each partner's goal is to design, but everyone understands that it is only by embracing aspects of business that some of their colleagues outside Pentagram might reject as boring (to their cost) that this ambition can be pursued effectively. The founding partners positioned the company with great deliberation to strike this balance. In 1983, five years after he had opened the New York office, Colin Forbes outlined the strategy. "There are design offices that are organized like advertising agencies, where design is a minor part of the process and the majority of principals are not designers," he said. "Then you have another group of firms that are dominated by designers. We belong to the latter group but believe we can organize ourselves better in a managerial

sense."[3] Pentagram would stake out a third position, novel in the American marketplace of the early 1980s, somewhere between the small, independent, creatively driven designers and unwieldy firms combining design and marketing. Its designer partners would communicate face to face with their corporate clients, without bothersome account executives and other go-betweens insufficiently versed in design thinking to defend design concepts with conviction when confronted by misunderstanding or resistance. Design would remain the object of the enterprise.

The strategy worked. Pentagram's clients by the mid-1980s included IBM, Olivetti, BP, Pirelli, Thorn EMI, Kodak, Polaroid, Clarks shoes, the Neiman Marcus stores, and British Rail. Their work was recognized for its wit, intelligence, elegance, clarity, and what one commentator called its "unequalled devotion to the idea of the idea."[4] Rather than aesthetic exploration and expression through form, this meant a preference for visual puns, rebuses, and other succinct visual devices, an approach derived from the type of visual thinking that came to dominate progressive American advertising and design in the 1950s. Alan Fletcher had spent time in the US, and Bob Gill was just one of a number of influential American designers active in London in the 1960s. The aim was to telegraph the message quickly and wittily without recourse to supposedly arbitrary, superfluous, and distracting stylistic effects. Consequently, as an observer noted, Pentagram design was rarely avant-garde: "It's mainstream, solid (some may describe it as 'safe') and Pentagram has a lot of solid, safe clients."[5]

In Pentagram's second book, *Living by Design* (1978), management theorist Peter Gorb suggests that no other design consultancy of the time had Pentagram's level of commitment to design. As a result, says Gorb, there was simply too much creativity for client needs, and this surplus manifested itself in the practice's style as an organization.[6] It was visible in Pentagram's flexible, functional, open-plan interior, in the collection of ethnic masks displayed on its exposed-brick walls, and in its imaginative publishing program. Pentagram was one of the first design companies in London to provide an in-house dining area for its staff. Design was not just a service supplied to clients; as their book title suggested, it was a calling, a style of being, a whole way of life. In the 1980s, client needs and expectations of what design might offer expanded tremendously, but the tension between what Pentagram had the potential to give its clients and what it was permitted to give them was always present. The more restrictive corporate jobs earn money that buys the freedom to pursue more personal, lower-paying work. (Pentagram partners are not alone in this regard—many designers undertake their share of "bread and butter" work.) However, founding partner Alan Fletcher left Pentagram in 1991 because he found himself taking on too many jobs that he did not wish to do, purely for the sake of income. "I really enjoy doing more personal work, as opposed to having to deal with large, complicated programs for clients," he told me. "It was difficult for me to do the sort of thing I wanted for that kind of project. I pulled it off a few times, but it's not so easy."[7]

Over time Pentagram has grappled with the problem of how to renew itself. The firm has evolved from its idealistic beginnings, through middle years of stable growth, to recent attempts to absorb more wayward and even "avant-garde" sensibilities. Peter Saville and April Greiman, two of the most original and influential graphic designers of the 1980s, were recruited to the partners' ranks, though neither relationship blossomed or lasted. Their departures demonstrate that finding personalities who can adapt themselves to Pentagram's ethos and structure requires considerable care. Daniel Weil, one of the 1980s' most visionary industrial-design thinkers, bonded successfully after joining the London office in 1992. Abbott Miller's decision to join New York in 1999, after a decade as high-profile designer, writer, and editor, was not only a sign that Pentagram had a broad-minded view of what qualities might add to its strength but also an indication that the firm was perceived by emerging young designers as a hospitable environment for challenging cultural projects.

Today, Pentagram has reinvigorated itself in a way that has few parallels among design practices. Firms with two or three partners tend to grow hoary with their principals. Even when they are groomed for the role, the next in line rarely attain the same stature and preeminence. If the founding partners' names also form the company name, this makes the dilemma even more obvious. Four of Pentagram's five founding partners—Fletcher, Forbes, Mervyn Kurlansky, and Kenneth Grange—have left the company, and Theo Crosby has died. Of the nineteen partners in spring 2003, McConnell joined in 1974, David Hillman in 1978, Kit Hinrichs in 1986, and Woody Pirtle in 1988. John Rushworth was the first partner to be promoted from associate, in 1989. The other fourteen partners have joined or, in two cases, have been promoted from within since 1990. Despite this now continuous process of renewal, "second-generation" Pentagram feels, in spirit, in its internal culture, and in its position in relation to other design companies, like a continuation of its founders' vision and aims. The wide range of fairly evenly spaced ages among the partners—from thirty-eight (Lisa Strausfeld) to sixty-four (McConnell) at time of writing—means that Pentagram could in theory renew itself indefinitely, without experiencing abrupt transitions or a sudden need to find replacements when partners decide to leave or older partners retire.

Pentagram's partnership structure is its single most remarkable idea. Strictly speaking, its principals are not really partners—they are directors and shareholders—but they use the term to convey the spirit of the relationship. McConnell has memorably described the practice as a collection of "19 kitchen tables."[8] When a new partner joins Pentagram, another kitchen table is added to the group. It's an attractively romantic image, intended to evoke the exhilarating early days of a young designer's career when there are few firm commitments, no burdensome overheads to interfere with creative choices, and everything to play for. According to conventional business wisdom, a company that seeks to grow should have a pyramid structure, with tiers of management and a leader at the top, and it should expand by acquiring other businesses. Pentagram's development, by contrast, is organic. It is driven by individuals, not by the dictates of the market. It grows horizontally, not vertically, in whatever direction suits the partners' wishes and preferences, and somehow it works. The Austin, Texas, office exists because partner Lowell Williams wanted to live there, rather than for any pressing strategic purpose.

Following spread: Pentagram Papers, *1975–present.*

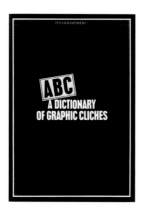

ABC
A DICTIONARY
OF GRAPHIC CLICHES

THE
PESSIMIST
UTOPIA

BRUSHES
AND

Face to face

THE PALACE
OF THE LEAGUE
OF NATIONS
AN
ARCHITECTURAL
COMPETITION
IN ITS SOCIAL
AND HISTORICAL
CONTEXT

WOULD YOU CARE
TO MAKE A
CONTRIBUTION?

PHOTOGRAPHS OF BOMARZO

Views from Pentagram, 212 5th Avenue, NY   Photographed by Bruce Davidson

Unilever House:
Towards
A New Ornament

1211 North LaSalle

The city of tomorrow:
model 1937

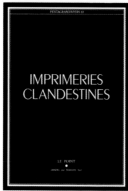

IMPRIMERIES
CLANDESTINES

LE POINT

STARS & STRIPES

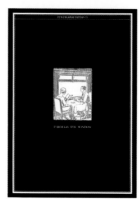

THROUGH THE WINDOW

KINGSWALDEN
NOTES

MCMLXX

THE MANY FACES OF MAN

SKELETON CLOSET

Purple, White and Green

Reading With a Purpose

ARCHITECTURE
By
LEWIS MUMFORD

1988

CROP CIRCLES

ARCHITECTURAL TOYS

The Arms of Paris

SOUVENIR ALBUMS

On Pride and Prejudice
in the Arts
SIR ERNST GOMBRICH, OM

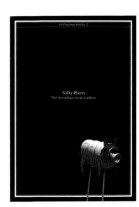

Nifty Places
The Australian rural mailbox

SAVOY

NEON-LIT
KIDNEY-SHAPED
LOW-RENT
FLAT-ROOFED
DOO-WOP
COMMERCIAL
ARCHITECTURE

NO WASTE

When Pentagram departed from this principle in the mid-1990s and opened an office in Hong Kong mainly because it seemed to make commercial sense, it proved to be a mistake, and they closed it after three years.

No other design company can boast Pentagram's concentration of fully engaged design horsepower at the highest operational level. Each partner is a separate profit center and recruits and manages his or her own team of designers while enjoying the benefits of shared central resources such as administration, accounts, and communications. Law practices and management consultancies have similar company structures, but the *Financial Times* was still moved to observe in 2002 that little that goes on at Pentagram would be found on an MBA course.[9] People sometimes ask whether there is any limit to the number of partners the company could absorb, and some partners believe that there is no limit, but the question is moot because Pentagram's rate of growth is actually quite modest. The total number of partners has increased by only three in the last ten years, even though the search for potential recruits goes on all the time. It is questionable, in any case, whether such a clubby and carefully balanced social organism could accommodate a big increase in the number of partners.

The origins of this model go back to the founding partners' experiences in the 1960s. A friend told Forbes that it would be possible to chart the course of their business in the years ahead and drew a graph. Forbes did not pay this much attention until he happened to look at the graph a few years later and found that its predictions about growth, turnover, and how many employees would be needed were correct. In collaboration with his client and mentor Ian Hay Davidson, then a partner at Arthur Andersen, Forbes devised Pentagram's cellular structure. At the core of the plan was the idea of equality. Each partner would receive the same salary and an equal share of annual profits. However, new partners usually start at a lower salary based on growth projected from the business they bring with them. During the period before they are fully vested, which is at least two years, partners-elect also receive a bonus based on their own profit. In order to lighten their financial load, incoming partners are able to buy shares at asset value only, without having to make a goodwill payment.

When Pentagram started, Forbes introduced the idea of partners' retreats, which would take place twice a year. These policy meetings have continued to this day—at venues such as the American Academy in Rome and the St. Francis Yacht Club in San Francisco—and they play an essential role in encouraging communication, especially across the Atlantic, cementing relationships and maintaining cohesion within the group. A series of commemorative photographs taken on these occasions, showing the growing band of partners posed in verdant fields, in picturesque country gardens, and on the steps of an Italian villa makes these retreats look more like holidays than work. Here again, it seems that Pentagram's longevity comes partly from maintaining a self-interested balance between business and pleasure. This hedonistic play principle, another seeming product of their 1960s origins, did not become widespread as an organizational philosophy until the 1990s, even in the design business. Partners present their work to each other at the meetings, and there is a chance to share knowledge and learn from each other's experiences—one of the fundamental aims and advantages of belonging to Pentagram. "I believe the meetings are one of the major reasons the partners have stayed together," writes Forbes.[10]

The role of chairing these meetings fell to Forbes, and he steered them for eighteen years. In 1991, when he announced his plan to resign, the other partners realized that there were aspects of leading a company that they knew little about. There was evidently a need to rethink Pentagram's constitution for the next decade. Forbes was advised that the chairman's tasks should remain in one person's hands, but after consultation with the partners, he proposed a structure that no conventional corporation would countenance. Three committees were formed: a policy committee, a finance committee, and a communications committee. The international policy committee was the governing body of the group. All partners and partners-elect were members, and the committee dealt with any matters of policy that were not covered by the other committees. One partner was elected as chairman and held the position for three meetings (eighteen months); then another partner would take over. Every partner had the opportunity to serve as chairman once he or she was sufficiently familiar with Pentagram's culture; the task would alternate between London and the US. The committee for finance consisted of one representative from each office, chosen locally, and an elected chairman. The communications committee had only two members— one from the US and one from the UK. After six months, it was decided that there should be an additional steering committee, constituted along the same lines and responsible for long-term strategic planning and for resolving internal conflicts. Today, there is also a "First Five" committee, a forum for the partners and partners-elect who have been in Pentagram for less than five years.

The handover period before Forbes withdrew in 1991 was clearly not easy. A line at the end of an article about this period of transition, published in 1992, records how hard he had found it to write and begs the partners' indulgence. "With changes, one is bound to make mistakes; things have fallen between the cracks and we have had to arrive at new definitions of responsibility," notes Forbes. "Designers must learn to be managers and to take executive responsibility or their company policy will be set by administrators."[11]

Pentagram's long life gives it an appearance of inevitability, but one only has to consider the difficulties inherent in such a transitional moment, with so much at stake, to be reminded that there is nothing inevitable about it. The creative freedom Pentagram partners enjoy is underpinned by careful strategic thinking and a close attention to organizational realities. What qualities, then, does it take to become one of Pentagram's "lofty, Olympian, benevolent despots"—as an observer once put it?[12] As part of his early 1990s review, Forbes stipulated four criteria:

- A partner must be able to generate business. Collaborative help and support is available, but each partner must take responsibility for finding projects.
- A partner must have a national reputation as an outstanding professional in his or her discipline.
- A partner must be able to control projects and contribute profits to the firm.
- A partner must be a proactive member of the group and care about Pentagram and the other partners.

The formal requirements do not, of course, tell the full story. A Pentagram partner will need to be outward going and sociable and to click with the group. McConnell puts this in the most basic terms: "Could you bear to spend a weekend with them?"[13] They will also need the confidence to stand up to being critiqued by fellow partners. In the studios, where they work close together, able to overhear one another's conversations and phone calls, they pass by each other's desks all the time, and everyone feels free to comment. "You can't get away with anything in here," Fletcher once remarked. "So the partnership acts as an irritating self-protection system."[14] These debates and the need to offer clearly thought-out rationales for creative decisions help to maintain standards of work. Partners must also be able to handle the constant pressure to perform financially. This is not directly imposed by other partners, who all face the same pressure, but comes from within. Each partner receives a monthly statement showing their sales, the costs of doing business, and their profit and loss, and a profitability report is presented at the twice-yearly partner meetings, so everyone knows how everyone else is doing. No partner wants to find him- or herself at the bottom of the profitability list for more than three years in a row. It is accepted by all partners that there are bound to be occasions when the benefits to Pentagram of undertaking a less profitable project compensate for any shortfall. A project might be prestigious, gain favorable press coverage, or contribute to perceptions of Pentagram as a producer of good design. As with so many aspects of the Pentagram experiment, it is a question of maintaining the right balance.

Milton Glaser observed many years ago that Pentagram was notable for its "sense of generosity," and this quality seems to lie at the heart of what the company has achieved and of its ability to renew itself. The partners' generosity extends first of all toward each other. "Generosity means that we respect one another's work and we share ideas and are willing to give one another the [financial] freedom we need," says Weil.[15] This is a fine thing for the partners, and it makes Pentagram a fascinating case study for students of organizational behavior, but if their generosity stopped with one another, it would not make Pentagram an

Pentagram Book Five. Fifty case histories in architecture, graphic, and industrial design from the international consultancy Pentagram

The Compendium

Pentagram

IDEAS ON DESIGN PENTAGRAM

Living by design. Pentagram

Pentagram

IDEAS

Pentagram:
the work of five designers
l'oeuvre de cinq designers
fünf Designer und ihre Arbeiten

Lund
Humphries
London

Whitney
Library of
Design
New York

Lund
Humphries

ff

exceptional design company. What is truly notable is the way this spirit of generosity informs Pentagram's entire approach to design. Observers are often fascinated by Pentagram's organizational peculiarities, but its ultimate purpose in configuring itself in this way has received less attention.

Pentagram's founders made no secret of their ambitions. As a foreword in their first book explained: "Though each is a specialist they are ambitious to be universal men, to grasp at opportunities outside their speciality and to use them to explode the bounds of that speciality."[16] This was said in 1972, and it is unlikely that anyone at Pentagram would use a phrase such as "universal men" today—it has an almost H. G. Wells-ian, science-fiction ring to it now—but the essential idea remains the same. Pentagram's founders conceived of design's role in the grandest terms, but they knew that however well-intentioned designers might be, on their own they are weak. They lack influence with clients, especially larger, more powerful clients, and they lack power and influence in society and politics. "The tragedy of the graphic design profession is that so many of its most talented practitioners are inarticulate, shy, or otherwise incapable of persuading larger groups of people that there is inherent value in design," writes Scher.[17] Modernist designers might once have visualized themselves as social progressives with the aesthetic vision to help shape a new kind of society, but in the late twentieth century, design occupied a more constrained and prosaic role, finding itself increasingly usurped by other kinds of demand and influence, above all from marketing. Banding together gave Pentagram's partners a collective strength that they could never have achieved on their own. It gave the company the appearance of size and adequate resources that is essential when dealing with large companies, and the experience the partners gained by working at this level made Pentagram a formidably persuasive force.

What is it, then, that Pentagram stands for? Over the years, the partners have shown little inclination

to pontificate about this, or if they have done so, their thoughts have only occasionally made it into print. In an interview in an architecture magazine in 1976, Forbes noted that their aim was to "try to improve the quality of industrial life," and Crosby added that they wanted to improve civic life, too.[18] A decade later, McConnell described how Pentagram sought to use its experience and skills "to make things happen for the increased benefit of the design community, the community at large and for us."[19] In Pentagram's fourth book, *The Compendium* (1993), McConnell returned to the theme of interconnectedness. He noted that Pentagram did not draw a distinction between the state of design culture and the state of the design business, and this, after all, is the essence of Pentagram's achievement—its effectiveness and durability as a business makes possible its enduring commitment to design. "Working for the design industry is really working for ourselves," concludes McConnell. "Disseminating our views, attitudes and knowledge to the wide audience ultimately helps our own business cause as well."[20]

Most of the time Pentagram has preferred to express this aim implicitly, through the work it produces rather than through explicit statements or manifestos. No design company has published books about itself with such frequency, but the primary aim has always been not to advance a program or espouse any particular cause but to show and perhaps illuminate some of the company's projects. The idealism that has marked Pentagram's thirty-year history can be seen, above all, in its dedication to the idea of "quality." This is a notion that would have passed without comment in design circles for much of Pentagram's first two decades. Standards of what constituted "good design" were determined by design's leading figures—a group to which Pentagram clearly belonged—and they were enshrined in the acquisition policies of modernist institutions such as the Museum of Modern Art and, more commercially, in the awards conferred by organizations such as the Art Directors Club in New York and Design & Art Direction (D&AD) in London. Good design was something that good designers, along with other people of refinement and good taste, instinctively recognized. In the 1990s, though, design, like other areas of cultural activity, was exposed to relentless

Left: Pentagram: The Work of Five Designers *(Lund Humphries, 1972),* Living by Design *(Lund Humphries, 1978),* Ideas on Design *(Faber & Faber, 1986),* The Compendium *(Phaidon Press, 1993), and* Pentagram Book Five *(The Monacelli Press, 1999).*

questioning. Now that postmodern relativism had become the norm, any particular design style or approach's claim to absolute rightness looked suspect. While Pentagram's London studio continues to produce design—especially graphic design—that broadly observes a modernist way of thinking, American Pentagram has a much more variegated output. Quality, in this context, can only mean "among the best of its kind," but even relativistic value judgments such as this require a new set of yardsticks. It is not yet certain how fully Pentagram has embraced these realities, and its continuing development as a vital force within design will depend, in part, on the sophistication with which it is able to evolve creative positions that are definite—we can see what they stand for—yet also nuanced, flexible and undogmatic.

Pentagram Papers, Pentagram's long-term publishing project, embodies the open-mindedness such an evolution will require. The publication presents readers with "examples of curious, entertaining, stimulating, provocative and occasionally controversial points of view" that have come to the partners' attention.[21] The thirty-one issues of the elegantly designed black booklet, first published in 1975, explore many intriguing and sometimes overlooked aspects of visual culture: the Suffragettes' use of design, French Underground printers during the Nazi occupation, architectural toys, crop circles, rural Australian mailboxes, American commercial architecture, and badges bearing the face of Mao Zedong. With notable generosity, Pentagram sends out 3,500 complimentary copies of every issue to people on its mailing list and gives away many more. While many design companies produce occasional publications and promotional giveaways, *Pentagram Papers*' editorial and curatorial seriousness and its consistency over time make it one of a kind. These highly collectible paeans to material culture and its informal influences on designing are a powerful reminder of Pentagram's lasting commitment to the culture of design.

In recent years, New York partners Michael Bierut and Paula Scher have been the most outspoken in trying to voice the idealism that underlies Pentagram's position. Bierut cites American designer William Golden, creator of the CBS eye logo, who wrote in 1959: "I happen to believe that the visual environment...improves each time a designer produces a good design—and in no other way."[22] As Bierut points out, midcentury American designers were committed to the idea that good design could be used as a tool to ameliorate and elevate the activities of everyday life. Designers in Europe shared the same ideal, and Pentagram's founders were educated in British art schools at a time when it was taken for granted by many in the profession that they carried a responsibility to help improve the visual environment for all. If designers committed to the pursuit of quality—loaded as this notion might have become—were to withdraw from this task, asks Bierut, what would happen to the fabric of the public realm? It would be left to decline and decay in the hands of those without the ability or motivation to do anything about it, and who would benefit then? Certainly not ordinary people. Pentagram's aim, notes Scher, is to try to raise the level and lift the intelligence of whatever area of design the partner confronts. "All things matter," says Scher. "Doing cultural institutions is not more important than doing corporations or restaurants—all of that adds to an enlightened society."

This is where Pentagram parts company with more uncompromising critics of design's role in the commercial realm. All designers are naturally excited by the first phase of the design process. This is the most creative part of the project. The designer examines the problem from every angle and explores many different directions. Inspired ideas emerge, and breakthroughs are made. Only if the designer can steer the project through the second phase, though, do these ideas stand any chance of coming to fruition. It is here, dealing with the client, that the designer faces the reality of the situation in all its behavioral, organizational, and economic complexity. The designer will try to retain as much phase-one thinking as possible, but some degree of compromise will almost certainly be required. The budget cannot stretch to cover a cherished idea. Planning regulations rule out a particular approach. Such compromises can be painful, and some designers, preferring to maintain their purity, never attempt to work for the kind of clients likely to make such demands. "It's depressing if one wants to be an idealist," says Scher. "On the other hand, what's more depressing is nothing ever getting better, from our point of view—that's our idealism. If you cannot produce the phase-two part, then you cannot affect the culture of society. That's the heart of it. To accomplish that requires influence and power, because if you have to make groups of people listen to you, believe in you, make change, overcome fear, invest money, then you have to be able to persuade them to move incrementally in a direction."

Scher's final thought—that change will be incremental—might seem anticlimactic to anyone whose spirits began to lift at the prospect of exerting a decisive influence on society. Design's discontents sometimes talk as though one massive, spontaneous push within the profession could transform design and overturn overnight the circumstances in which it operates. They never trouble to explain how in any practical sense such an impulse could arise, because they are dreaming aloud, with no real hope of transforming anything. Pentagram may not be a fired-up corporate agitator, demanding revolutionary change, but its doggedly patient strategy of incremental gain is certainly realistic in its awareness of the flawed human situations in which design must struggle to find its place. Over the course of three decades, the partners have offered fellow designers a convincing model of how this can work. It is astonishing that more have not tried the same strategy. For any designer who hopes to build a responsive, long-lasting and influential form of practice, the idea of Pentagram deserves the closest study.

1. Quoted in Graham Vickers, "Joining Forces," *Creative Review*, October 2000, 41.
2. Paula Scher, *Make it Bigger*, New York: Princeton Architectural Press, 2002, 162.
3. Quoted in Patricia Leigh Brown, "The Americanization of Pentagram," *Metropolis*, March 1983, 13.
4. Jenny Towndrow, "Pentagram," *Graphics World*, September 1987, 55.
5. *Ibid*.
6. Peter Gorb ed., *Living by Design*, London: Lund Humphries/New York: Whitney Library of Design, 1978, p. 287.
7. Quoted in "Rick Poynor in conversation with Alan Fletcher," in Jeremy Myerson et al., *Beware Wet Paint: Designs by Alan Fletcher*, London: Phaidon, 1996, 61.
8. Quoted in Tim Rich, "The Art of Partnership," *How*, December 2000, 79.
9. Fiona Harvey, "Equals to the Task," *FT Creative Business*, 8 January 2002, 8.
10. Colin Forbes, "Transition," *Communication Arts Design Annual*, 1992, 261.
11. *Ibid.*, 262–3.
12. Towndrow, 57.
13. Quoted in Vickers, 40.
14. Quoted in Rick Poynor, "Alan Fletcher," Eye, Winter 1991, 11.
15. Quoted in Harvey, 9.
16. *Pentagram: The Work of Five Designers*, London: Lund Humphries, 1972, 1.
17. Scher, 164.
18. Quoted in John McKean, "Pentagram: The Magic Formula for Design?" *Building Design*, January 1976.
19. Towndrow, 61.
20. John McConnell in David Gibbs ed., *The Compendium*, London: Phaidon, 1993, 260.
21. From a statement published on the cover flap of all issues of *Pentagram Papers*.
22. Quoted in Michael Bierut, "A Manifesto with Ten Footnotes," *I.D.*, March/April 2000, 79. See William Golden, "Visual Environment of Advertising" in Michael Bierut et al. eds., *Looking Closer Three: Classic Writings on Graphic Design*, New York: Allworth Press, 1999, 130–4.

Following six spreads: The international partners' meeting, New York, November 2003.

Working from the Inside Out

Lance Knobel on *John McConnell*

MANY DESIGN GROUPS DELUDED THEMSELVES over the last fifteen years. Not content with design, they positioned themselves as strategic consultancies, hired fresh-faced MBAs, and convinced themselves that they were competing with McKinsey and Bain. Instead of being shunted off with a client's marketing or product managers, they would gain access to the holy of holies, the CEO. Design has moved on, and it's safe to say that the McKinseys of the world never even knew about the upstart pretenders.

Pentagram never had its head turned by these pretensions. It contented itself with "just" designing, pursuing work that appealed to partners and not dreams of IPOs or acquisitions. For that, some credit can be given to the original spirit of the practice, embodied in many ways by John McConnell, a Pentagram partner since 1974. Like the original five partners, McConnell is happy to be seen as a humble toiler in the fields of design. When he discusses his career, he is proud of his blue-collar design origins—entering art school in Maidstone at age fourteen and working in Dublin and London before opening his own business at age twenty-four. In today's Pentagram, without the founding five partners, McConnell is very much a keeper of the flame, actively guaranteeing that the original ethos is retained as new partners enter the practice.

When you talk to McConnell about design, the phrases that constantly recur are common sense, clarity, and simplicity. His designs tend to have simple, almost naive ideas at their heart. Take two themes that McConnell finds particularly interesting: faces and repetition. Before he joined Pentagram, McConnell was a founder of the typesetting company Face. For many years, he designed an annual calendar for the firm which played with countless variations of a face. He returned to faces in his work for the Barcelona-based confectioners Joyco, where both the logo and the bubble-gum wrappers became graphic faces. There is a charming literalness in using faces for the identity (and perhaps an echo of the round bubbles blown with Joyco gum), a sweetness apparently not lost on the Spanish confectioner.

McConnell explains the appeal of repetition as the "tin-soldier principle." He recalls going into toy

Opposite: Mark for the Japan 2001 festival, London, 2000.

42

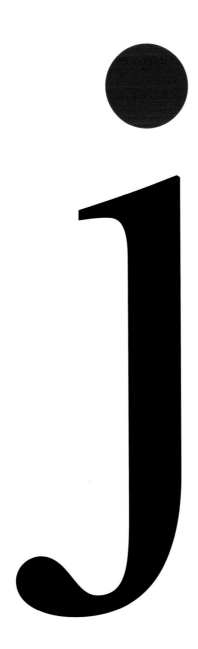

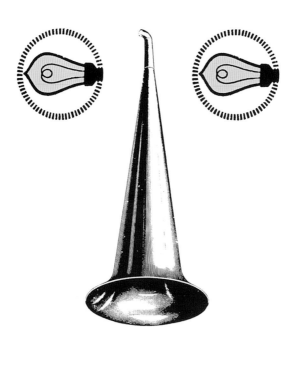

shops as a child and being fascinated by the rows of tin soldiers. But scraping together the money to buy just one was hugely disappointing. The joy came through having the whole row of soldiers. The tin-soldier principle accounts for the appeal of window displays at department store John Lewis, a new client of McConnell's, which might consist of just a row of washing machines. This may be one of the most productive (and lucrative) uses of the inner child since psychologists gave birth to the idea.

His attitude toward design echoes a distinction that was made in a radically different field, by the economic historian Joel Mokyr: "The important difference between technology and magic is not that technology works and magic does not," Mokyr writes. "The difference that matters here is that magic does not control nature, it begs favors from it. Rather than exploiting regularities and natural laws, it seeks exceptions to them by taking advantage of an imaginary capriciousness of the universe. Moreover, technology, if it worked, worked for everyone, whereas magic was confined to qualified practitioners."

For technology, read design as it is understood by McConnell. For magic, read the kind of indulgent, tricky design that he rejects. (There is, of course, a magic that he pursues, the alchemy of ingredients that makes a design memorable.) His design always works within the grain of regularities and natural laws rather than the capricious. And much of McConnell's work is about creating structures and processes that enable a good result whoever is doing the actual design work: It works, and works for everyone.

So there is a nonmystical approach that meshes with the preference for the direct and simple. But if McConnell favors simplicity and shudders at the idea of design as management consultancy, there's a paradox. Within the practice and within the strongly held bounds of partner equality, McConnell is very much the management partner, watching costs and revenues. And the bulk of his work in recent years has been precisely at the intersection of

*Left: Naming and mark for a Spanish-based international confectionery group, 1999. **Opposite:** Portrait of Thomas Edison, one of twelve from a calendar designed for typesetting company Face, 1988.*

design and management. In 1981 he created a new identity and design template for publishers Faber & Faber. That led to a fifteen-year association with Faber (including seven years as a board director), using his clout in the senior management to ensure the design standards permeated the firm.

He similarly was design director of Boots, the UK's largest chain of pharmacies, for nearly twenty years. When Boots approached McConnell years ago seeking a rule book for design, he said he would provide not a design solution but a management one (without an MBA in sight). He explained to the Boots board that standard design approaches were inadequate. "You could paint all the packs blue and have lots of synergy and no business. Or you could source the packaging design work from one design firm to create a synergy, and you would fall out in five minutes and the internal politics would defeat them."

McConnell proposed introducing instead a new system of purchasing design to use many different design talents and make key decisions at a much higher level within the company. As at Faber, he would be on the inside, ensuring core principles about the brand were enforced and steering and guiding work. "You can't change an organization fundamentally from the outside," McConnell explains, "and certainly not by putting up boards of pretty visuals. You have to get inside and change the way things are looked at."

This judgment was arrived at precisely because of frustration built up over the years at working from the outside. It curiously parallels contemporary thinking about management. The big strategic consultancies, like McKinsey, Boston Consulting, and Bain, have tried to shift away from working on a single project, the result of which is a fat report for the CEO (although for a price, they will still do precisely that). The preference is for a continuing engagement, where the consultancy can insinuate itself into an organization and work from the inside to achieve transformation.

As implemented, McConnell's approach to design management attacks what he terms the "pyramids" of a typical retailer. Product managers are at the apex of the pyramid, while designers—typically quite junior—labor at the bottom. So designs are commissioned and executed far down the

organization, and each buying department takes its own approach.

McConnell's solution bypasses those pyramids by creating a design-policy group just below board level to vet design briefs and concept solutions agreed upon by product managers and external designers. It moves decisions, he says, "from the ankles to the brain."

In this model, external designers, chosen by McConnell from outside Pentagram's ranks, can become part of what he calls the "family." Members of the family come to understand the common "handwriting" that gives a sense of a client's identity. The handwriting is not the set of design rules: In the case of the work for Boots pharmacies, the only rules concerned the use of the Boots lozenge and the preferred Boots shade of blue. The handwriting is more to do with the deep sense of the brand. For Boots, McConnell defined this as "the man in the white coat, the nation's chemist." This implied trustworthiness, intelligence, integrity, straight-forwardness, and professionalism (echoes, in fact, of everything McConnell likes in design). In design terms, it precluded anything modish, aggressive, or seemingly cut-price.

McConnell works in the middle, steering the client's design choices and supporting the family of designers. He can prove a both benign and strict godfather to the family. When designers are being stymied in their work by a client's product team, they learn to have a quiet word with McConnell. Then, when the work appears at the design-policy group, McConnell can ask the designers whether they have a different treatment to show. Equally, when designers aren't proving up to scratch, they don't remain in the family fold.

He is adamant about avoiding any conflict between his role in design management and the detailed design itself. McConnell insists that is essential to maintain credibility with the design suppliers. "You can't conduct the orchestra and be a soloist at the same time," he says. Could McConnell's own love of the actual craft of design be frustrated on the

Opposite: Book-jacket design for Faber & Faber. From top to bottom: Fiction, Poetry, Film, Plays, and Contemporary Classics (Plays), 1981–96.

XPOster '97: 12 Designer aus 12 Ländern für
die Weltausstellung EXPO 2000 in Hannover Design: John Mc Connell, Pentagram, Great Britain

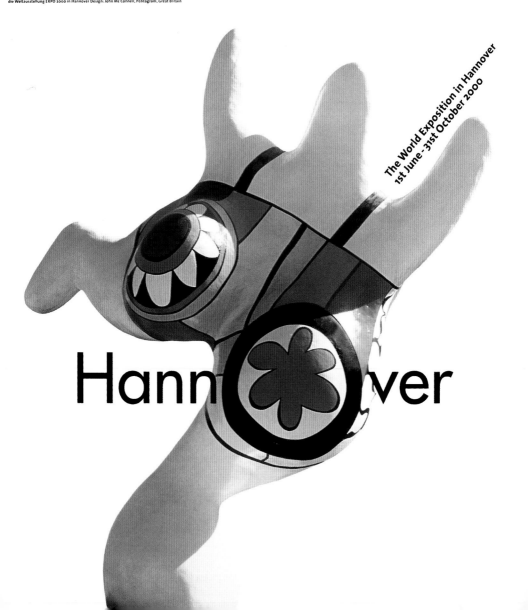

The World Exposition in Hannover
1st June - 31st October 2000

Hann*over

NAPOLI

A poster commissioned by
NAPOLI 99 Foundation as a contribution
towards the cultural image of the city

Never
Knowingly
Undersold

John Lewis Account

John Lewis

Account card
Application form

John Lewis

Account card
Your copy of
our agreement

John Lewis

Account card
Why pay
by direct debit?

John Lewis

conductor's podium? He emphasizes the excitement of creating a process that produces good results. "A great piece of work is there because you enabled it."

McConnell is now implementing his method with the John Lewis Partnership—the retailing group whose stores feature the repetitive washing-machine displays McConnell so admires. John Lewis is a group with a proud design tradition of its own and a cooperative whose ethos fits easily with Pentagram's own design philosophy. The great British designers Robin and Lucienne Day were in charge of design at John Lewis in the 1950s, producing successful and innovative furniture and textile designs. But their work tended to focus on individual projects rather than the whole, commercial picture. Lucienne Day, for example, once decided it would be interesting to commission artists to paint warehouse garage doors. McConnell would rather put the effort and investment into works that affect the customer.

It's not that McConnell doesn't appreciate Day's beautiful garage doors. Yet for him, that's not design,

which in his view requires a commercial impulse. He enjoys citing American designer Paul Rand, who believed good design required the "integration of the beautiful and the useful." McConnell thrives on the pressure and resistance of a fee provider. So strong is this conviction that he claims he never regrets discarding ideas that don't win client approval. McConnell is more interested, he says, in the results than in the design. Unrealized work might as well not exist.

The paradox of John McConnell perhaps displays the enduring strengths of the Pentagram model. On the one hand, he holds strongly to the craft of design, often referring back to the original notion of an applied art, two words that have always sat in productive tension. He constantly seeks to simplify, to clear the messy undergrowth that clutters the view so a strong idea can shine through. On the other hand, he feels comfortable in the boardroom and has as strong a commitment to profitable results as any of his client CEOs. And McConnell admits to reveling in a certain kind of power. "There's great satisfaction in getting into a position where you are listened to, and where you can get people to work in the same direction."

Opposite: Graphic device identifying a retail proposition for John Lewis department stores, 2002. Above: Set of financial services brochures for John Lewis department stores, 2002.

The Choreography
of Site-Specific Media

Janet Abrams on *Lisa Strausfeld*

PENTAGRAM MADE A VERY SHREWD MOVE when it brought Lisa Strausfeld on board in January 2002. With her appointment, the firm brought into its ranks an alumna of the 1990s-era Visible Language Workshop at MIT's Media Lab, and thus one of the elite corps from a program whose influence is already proving disproportionate to its graduates' actual numbers and relative youthful careers.[1]

Strausfeld's résumé includes a hybrid education encompassing art history and computer science at Brown University, followed by a master's degree in architecture from Harvard. Only then did she move "down the block" to the MIT Media Lab. It was there that I first encountered her in 1994, while I was conducting what turned out to be the last interview with her professor Muriel Cooper, the eccentric but brilliant director of the Lab's Visible Language Workshop.[2]

Strausfeld's arrival at the Media Lab coincided with the donation of several powerful new Silicon Graphics computers capable of generating three-dimensional information "spaces." "There was a serendipitous convergence: We got the first batch of SGIs, so it was the first time anyone in the VLW had worked in three dimensions," something which, fresh from architecture grad school, made perfect sense to her. She became interested in the structure of information, the abundant spatial metaphors we employ to denote our daily activities, and their possible computational equivalents.

Strausfeld has continued to work at the frontiers of interactive design, through several career phases. After graduating from MIT, she established Perspecta, a San Francisco-based software-development company with two fellow Media Lab graduates, Earl Rennison and Nicolas Saint-Arnaud. She decided to leave that company even before the dot-com bubble burst, to join Quokka Sports, where, as director of its research arm, Quokka Labs, she developed prototypes for new ways of presenting live sports information on the Web. Shortly before Quokka's collapse in 2000, she moved to New York and went solo under her own

Opposite: Set design and projections for the off-Broadway play Snatches, *a docu-comedy by Laura Strausfeld based on the recorded conversations between Monica Lewinsky and Linda Tripp, summer 2001.*

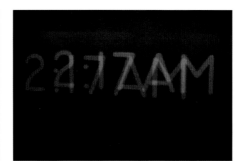

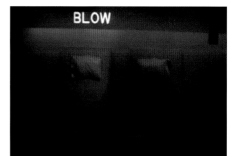

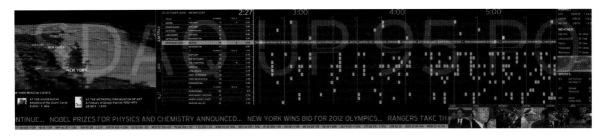

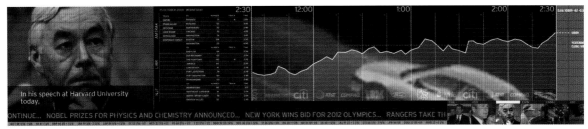

banner of InformationArt, working as a consultant to Pentagram to design a media wall for the new Pennsylvania Station in the renovated Farley Post Office building in midtown Manhattan.

In all these phases, Strausfeld has shown an abiding concern for the relationship between architectural space and information space and for the reinterpretation and reapplication of the precepts of architectural modernism to the realm of data. Recently she has begun to turn back to architectural space per se, with commissions to "embed" information into actual buildings: among them the aforementioned Penn Station; a transportation hub at the World Trade Center (commissioned by the Port Authority of New York and New Jersey before Studio Daniel Libeskind won the Ground Zero rebuilding commission); and the expansion of the Walker Art Center in Minneapolis, designed by the Swiss architects Herzog & de Meuron. Of these, the first two were designed as speculative prototypes and are now unlikely to be built; the third is slated for implementation in 2005.

In all three cases, Strausfeld demonstrates a methodological approach markedly in contrast to

Above and opposite: Media Wall prototype for the proposed redevelopment of Pennsylvania Station at the James A. Farley Post Office building in New York, 2000.

typical "information architecture," a term she hates using because of its connotations of commercial interactive design. Imbued with her architectural training, she treats each commission as a "problem" and information as "site-specific"—to be experienced bodily rather than just through the eyes (and fingertips).

The clues to this structural approach are revealed in a diagram she developed at Quokka, a grid showing the different degrees of "immersive" experience offered by different display devices. Screen dimensions are charted against durations of engagement and their various social contexts: from the individual experience of the handheld device or desktop computer to the more convivial group setting in an arena beholding a Jumbotron or other large-scale display. The diagram pinpoints Strausfeld's concern with the physical as well as with the emotional dimensions of experience. "The idea of embodying information has always been interesting to me. I like the idea of merging these two worlds—the world of abstract and intangible ideas, and the world of physical things."

At Perspecta, she and her partners developed information structures that allowed viewers to "fly through" information so that, as you moved "closer" to a particular piece of information, more and more detail, or related articles, came into view. While Perspecta's clients were mostly in the technology-news sector, she and Rennison also developed a

more contemplative demo, the Millennium Project, which arrayed landmark early-twentieth-century events in science, art, and politics as "information objects" suspended in black "virtual space" according to their longitude, latitude, and date. When these seemingly neutral colored specks were approached, explanatory text would come into focus, like wall labels hanging free of their walls. The resulting "ride" was reminiscent of trailers for movies set in outer space—implying an infinite depth of knowledge available for discovery.

Moving to Quokka, Strausfeld, a self-confessed non-sports fan, made it her goal "to capture every emotion of live sports events through data" rather than through the typical pictorial means: photos of vanquished or triumphant athletes. "It was about giving the driest data an emotional content." Here, instead of using implied three-dimensional deep space to "contain" rich troves of data, Strausfeld and her team concentrated on montaging different species of information, in variegated bands and boxes, across the plane of the Web page. Bucketloads

of numbers (the nutrients on which sports fans nourish themselves) offered every conceivable measurement—racers' positions, times, distances, and route cross sections, for example. Syncopated against these statistics, several windows of live streamed video from the racecourse (cameras mounted on, say, a Tour de France bicycle or Grand Prix race car) offered a dizzying multiplicity of vantage points. Compounded by techno sound tracks and interviews with the heroes themselves, reliving their own first-person experience in "replay" mode, the choreography of time and space had a vertiginous, seductive beauty.

The overall effect of these dense but riveting charts was to elevate sports to the status of medical emergency—trauma as entertainment—with patients' vital signs urgently and anxiously monitored. With options to toggle between alternate overviews, users gained a sense of pseudocontrol over the data—a

---

Above: Information "media stream" for prototype of a transportation terminal at the former site of the World Trade Center, 2002.

56

panoptic position more akin to that of a sports producer in a TV control room, deftly selecting which sources of live feed to broadcast.

For Strausfeld, though, it's not just numbers that count. Just as the site is of critical significance in generating architecture, so is the siting of information within a physical landscape: not for her the gigantic, one-size-fits-all electronic display board, indiscriminately blaring out public information and advertising. Instead, she analyzes the architectural environment and makes "site-specific" interventions, modulating the support structures on which media will be presented so they become kinetic sculptures that just happen to deliver information—from the necessary but banal (train times), to the apparently vital but largely ritualistic (stock-market figures), to the sublime but usually underfunded (e.g., public art projects, to whose presentation the "off hours" on the Penn Station and WTC media walls were earmarked).

If constructed, this monumental, two-hundred-foot long video screen would have been the dominant focus of this gigantic train-station concourse—one of our few remaining archetypes of public gathering spaces, besides the sporting arena and the airport. In lectures, Strausfeld frequently shows archive images of crowds in Times Square and Grand Central Station, assembled to watch epochal events like the first space shot: She is particularly interested in how the *collective* experience of news shapes social space. The Penn Station Media Wall is an expression of a (perhaps nostalgic) desire to create an information "hearth" that could connect myriad strangers, momentarily joined by their need to reach assorted destinations; here, however, multiple "story lines" deliberately disperse the viewers' attention rather than focus them on a single commanding narrative.

On the dominant upper proportion of the screen, train departure times alternate with vast dynamic graphs of stock-market data. A sliding-panel effect allows one type of information to give way to another or, concertina-like, to expand outward to fill the full real estate, in a gliding motion reminiscent of shuffled theatrical flats. Talking-head interviews are relayed on the upper left at Gulliveresque scale, while the obligatory stock-market ticker chatters away on the lower margin and several smaller video feeds are shown lower right. Giant letters, spelling NASDAQ and other totemic acronyms, appear now and again on the main body of the wall, scrolling right to left over static data in smaller point sizes. Diaphanous curtains of information glide over one another, transparent, hierarchical, and strenuously factual but somehow also miragelike, dreamy, and intangible—befitting the (numerical, and predominantly financial) contents.

Perhaps this is why the Penn Station Media Wall has become a canonical work without ever having been built: It is, in the nicest sense, vaporware, a work of "paper (information) architecture" whose dynamic dancing data and kaleidoscopic dazzle incarnate the zeitgeist fantasy of an endless upward stock market—a visible representation of the frenzied advances of technology—importing the adrenaline rush and sensory overload of the floor of the New York Stock Exchange to the hall of a major transit hub. It perfectly captures the boomtown mood of late-1990s dot-com New York—a theme park, as one E*Trade advert of the time unapologetically put it, in which "The Theme Is Money."

Postcrash and post-9/11, the attitude to technology has changed. Pentagram was invited by the Port Authority of New York and New Jersey to develop an information system for a transportation terminal on the World Trade Center site. Here, the data have slipped their moorings on the Big Board: Strausfeld threads a ribbonlike "media stream" (an eighteen-inch-wide, high-resolution LED display) through the terminal's spaces, winding, bending, and curving along walls, overhead, or potentially even on floors. Moving at different speeds and in different directions, the interactive text and graphics "accompany" people walking through the space and anticipate their needs (providing imminent transit departures, distances to food concessions; weather advisories followed by ads for nearby rainwear stores). For consistency, each category of information is kept in the same type size and horizontal position within the "stream."

A grove of slim, seventy-foot-high obelisks rises from the floor of the main terminal hall toward the upper retail balconies. These are positioned in the space in conjunction with three low, rectangular video "partitions," with the spare, space-making intent of minimalist sculpture (Strausfeld is particularly admiring of Richard Serra's work). Branchless trees or dynamic totem poles, these programmable towers might, depending on the time of day, display the sound waves of arriving trains, carry local, civic, and national affairs, weather, or financial news, or simply serve as a bar-chart floor directory. Approached by visitors, the lowest six feet of each tower act as an interactive terminal, with further information about the actively displayed content or sponsor; after peak hours, when most "eyeballs" have caught their trains home, the towers would be released for public art presentations. Programmed collectively, advertisers might allow slivers of luxury brands to climb all five towers in sync, or show catwalk models in teasing partial glimpses that encourage the viewer to "fill in" missing information. Instead of revealing all, Strausfeld plays with the metonymic possibilities of commercial messages, sliced and diced as visual spectacle.

Indeed, her interests are increasingly turning toward the choreography of content. A diagram in Pentagram's WTC project documentation confirms this: An at-a-glance "score" of all the types of content that might be displayed during a typical twenty-four-hour schedule, it looks just like digital film-editing or music-authoring software, with multiple bands synchronized in a horizontal array. This chart "flattens out" the spatial differences between, say, the content in the West Concourse and the media walls in the Terminal Hall and strips away the semiotic complexities to reveal how much the meaning—the cognitive effect—of this system results above all from the syncopated *disjunctures* between different types of content, both horizontally (changing over time) and vertically (relative to one another, at a given moment). While Strausfeld recognizes the discrete iconic significance of different species of information (e.g., commercial advertising versus news versus public art images), the elegance and economy of this diagram suggest

Opposite: Prototype for dynamic displays of financial information for the new Bloomberg LP headquarters in New York, to be completed 2005.

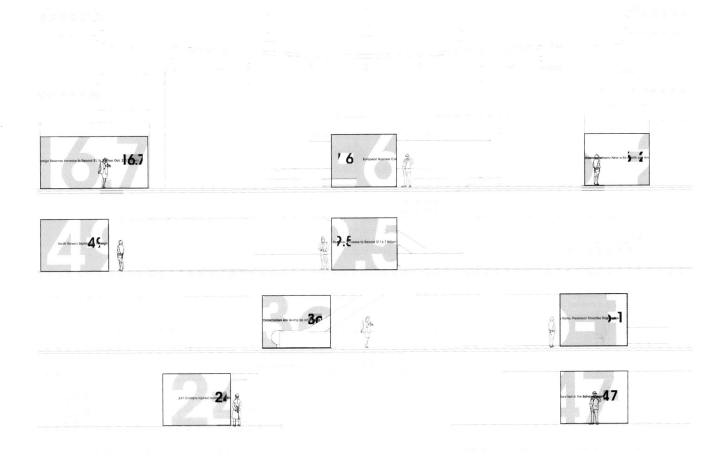

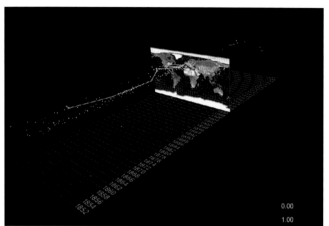

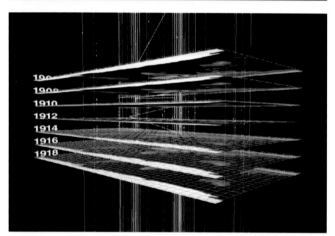

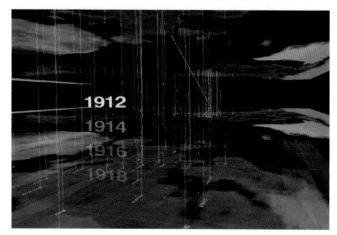

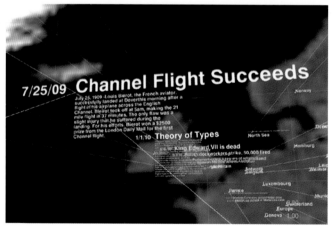

that, for her, what really matters is the overall orchestration of these media "channels" in time and space as a dynamic, site-specific system: that herein lies the relatively untapped potential of media in public spaces.

In the Walker Art Center proposal, Strausfeld takes an even more subtle and adventurous step toward her ambition eventually to "break free of the constraints of display. I'm interested in the work becoming independent of technology at some point: informed by it but not necessarily delivered by it."

Working with/in response to Herzog & de Meuron's architecture, Strausfeld eschews display panels in obvious places in favor of a hierarchy of information outlets. Whether these are gigantic letters projected onto a translucent exterior facade, or flat-screen monitors in the reception, or interactive wall panels announcing an artist's talk, or small, stealthy baseboard-level room-label displays, these nevertheless "speak" with a consistent institutional authority. "I like the idea that people think of the information as independent of any display, as a voice—the voice of the Walker—that's pushing information toward you, whether outside as you're driving to it, or inside. It's the difference between designing a banner for an institution and designing a sequence of banners that vary depending on where you are in the building, the time of day, and the kind of work on show."

Strausfeld sees herself moving toward editorial content development through the application of rule-based systems that "encode some kind of ambiguity in the best sense." Lately, teaching in the graphic design master's program at the Yale University School of Art, Strausfeld has instructed her thesis students to study the communication landscape along Route 22 in New Jersey, the suburban environment where she grew up. And she has inevitably found herself revisiting the work of Venturi, Scott Brown, and Izenour, whose *Learning from Las Vegas* of 1972 became a kind of holy writ about media in the urban environment, one now sorely due for updating.[3]

Cognizant of Venturi et al., but (thirty years on) with new tools, new densities of data, and the added dimension of interactivity to contend with, Strausfeld aims to create information experiences that have the lean but implicit richness of certain kinds of architecture—imbued with "moments of clear ambiguity," as she paradoxically describes it: "Before I even studied architecture formally, I was into the aesthetics of programming software. The most elegant solution to coding an algorithm was the shortest, the one with the fewest lines. There's a connection with architecture, where you design this artifact that doesn't move, this fixed thing that has to accommodate all these activities over time. Designing that elegant piece of code, designing a building that's the most essential form to accommodate all those activities: There's a certain design ethic about that, and an aesthetic that I admire."

1. Her MIT classmates included David Small, Grace Colby, Suguru Ishizaki, and Yin Yin Wong.
2. Janet Abrams, "Muriel Cooper's Visible Wisdom," *I.D. Magazine*, September-October 1994. Strausfeld's use of very clean, mostly sans-serif typography and an elemental color palette worthy of Johannes Itten reflect both her architectural training and the abiding graphic influence of Cooper, who, as head of the media department at the MIT Press in the 1970s, designed the authoritative textbook on the Bauhaus and disdained the curlicues of postmodernist graphics as she reared a new generation of visual (interactive) designers.
3. Muriel Cooper also designed the original, 1972 edition of *Learning from Las Vegas*.

Opposite: The Millennium Project, a custom software database visualization of people, significant events, and artifacts from the early twentieth century, developed at the MIT Media Lab, 1995.

Picture Story

Emily King on *Angus Hyland*

I HAPPENED ON A CACHE of stray photographs during a recent run along North London's Grand Union Canal. I didn't stop to look at them. They seemed too forlorn to withstand scrutiny, but slowing my pace a little, I caught images of Japanese twenty-somethings enjoying communal high jinx in the ill-kempt surroundings typical of London's rental accommodation. I saw the pictures again on several subsequent runs, getting grubbier and sadder by the hour until eventually the local authorities took pity and cleared them away. These snaps weren't special, but they have stayed with me a lot longer than I would have expected. There is nothing more bereft than an uncherished photograph, an image that has been unmoored from its proper place and sent spinning in the sphere of unwarranted interpretation. Left loitering by a canal, pictures of cheerful young people become suggestive of violence and tragedy, although, in truth, they imply nothing more perturbing than a snatched purse.

The matchless sense of pathos summoned by found photographs has proved a rich seam of artistic substance. Christian Boltanski is the leading exponent of rescued-image melancholia, known or chewing up photographic specificity and regurgitating poetic generality. The work of Boltanski and his ilk offers migrant pictures lodgings but denies them a home. Hung in clean white cubes, the photographs are absorbed into art but remain utterly lost, their emotive quality relying on their apparent rootlessness. On a gallery wall, sometimes illuminated by a little candle, a portrait becomes a shrine regardless of the status of its subject. It's a clever trick, and it succeeds nearly every time, but I can't help feeling that it isn't quite right, that more regard should be paid to meaning.

In the face of such indeterminacy, it is a relief to turn to the work of Angus Hyland. Like the legions of found-image artists, he scours photographic archives for compelling pictures, but unlike them he creates a space where photographs can be true to themselves while being part of something else. Rather than diminishing images when placing them

Opposite: Catalog for Picture This: Contemporary Illustration from London, *a touring British Council exhibition curated by Angus Hyland, 2002.*

62

PICTURE THIS.

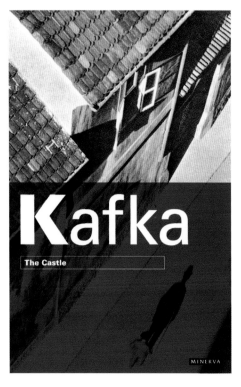

on book jackets, Hyland creates literary frames that enhance words and pictures alike. In an essay called "Fire and Ice," the critic Peter Wollen compares film's molten nature to photography's glacial core. Where would literature fit on this spectrum of elements? Could it be akin to air? Applying a photograph, anonymous or otherwise, to a book involves pairing the indeterminate and ethereal with the singular and apparent. It is very hard to do well, and contemporary bookshops are rife with word/image incongruity. The key to Hyland's unusual success in this tricky field lies in the considered choice of imagery. His intent focus on the content of both photography and literature leads him to pictures so appropriate that alternatives become unimaginable. In Hyland's hands the twinning of manuscript and image is made to appear easy.

Hyland began designing book covers soon after leaving the Royal College of Art in 1988. Working mainly for Minerva, he became part of a publishing production line, turning out two or three jackets a week. Many of the covers from this era are gathered in Hyland's pre-Pentagram portfolio, a small plastic snapshot album that he would allow clients to flick through. Looking at this album, it is obvious that much of Hyland's early work has more to do with the turnover speed and the clamorous influence of graphic history than his own creative vision. These layered, hand-drawn, color-flushed productions are often lovely but do not truly reflect Hyland's unique sensibility. In the graphic noise are several covers that speak more clearly, and these are the ones that indicate the direction that Hyland has taken in recent years. Shedding unwieldy graphic style, he has developed an approach that Canongate publisher Jamie Byng describes as "contemporary, minimalist and pure."

Hyland's first emphatic demonstration of his ability to pick up a picture and put it down in just the right place was the Minerva Kafka series. Published in 1992, these editions have a uniform identity, consisting of a translucent red strip across the lower half

Top left: Book jacket for Franz Kafka's The Castle, *published by Minerva, 1992.* **Left:** Book jacket for Sylvia Smith's Misadventures, *published by Canongate, 2001.* **Opposite:** Book jacket for Toni Davidson's Scar Culture, *published by Canongate, 1999.*

SCAR CULTURE

of each book that holds the author's name writ large and the book's title contained in a modestly sized rectangular lozenge. Beyond this identity, every volume in the series carries a different photographic image. My particular favorite is *The Castle*, which bears a picture of Prague by Czech photographer Josef Sudek. This cover is a straightforward case of finding a photograph a proper home. Sudek had lost an arm fighting in the trenches during World War I and, like Kafka, he was ambivalent toward authority. The image used by Hyland was taken only two years after the author's death and shows the streets of Prague from the perspective of the city's castle. The imbalance of power implied by the relative scales of the figure on the ground and the buttressed walls of the castle expresses the spirit of the novel. In an essay concerning the retrospective use of documentary photography, the artist and critic Martha Rosler expresses the fear that "topicality drops

away as epochs fade, and the aesthetic aspect is… enhanced by loss of specific reference."[2] Using Sudek's photograph nearly seventy years on, Hyland stems the outward flow of topicality and avoids vacant aestheticism through attention to provenance.

Hyland was able to develop his instinct for photographic meaning to the full in the Pocket Canon series, a collection of small paperback editions of core biblical texts, each introduced by a well-known author. The series was realized by the Edinburgh-based independent publishing house Canongate, and Jamie Byng was so sure of the originality and aptness of his project that, at the outset, he attempted to keep its exact nature secret. Visiting London studios in search of a designer, he arrived at Hyland's Soho base and was stunned by the power and simplicity of the Kafka covers. Elliptical discussions ensued, and, in spite of Byng's unwillingness to reveal the nature of his enterprise, Hyland proved himself the person for the job. With Hyland's contribution, the Pocket Canons became one of the biggest stories in British publishing of the late 1990s. Coming out

Below and opposite: Book jackets from the second series of the Pocket Canons, published by Canongate, 1999.

in 1998 and 1999 in two box sets, of twelve and nine volumes respectively, they overturned the conventions of religious publishing, placing well-worn words in a wholly unexpected context.

The starting point of the Pocket Canons series was the cover for the book of Revelation. Partnering Will Self's bleak personal introduction with a René Burri photograph of a mushroom cloud, Hyland expressed the sum of the twentieth century's public and private tragedies in a single image (an apocalyptic choice of image Hyland describes self-deprecatingly as "bleedin' obvious"). Covers in the series range from the literal—Helge Skodvin's long and winding road for the book of Exodus—to the metaphorical—the exploding house by Iranian photographer Abbas for Isaiah. The design of these books required Hyland to operate at a different scale than before. No longer able to search single-handedly through the mass of imagery, he had to rely on the help of two assistants and entire teams of picture-library researchers. Artist/writer Allan Sekula has described archives as "the clearing houses of photographic meaning."[3] Creating the Pocket Canons, Hyland became a trader of sorts, absorbed in extensive negotiations between textual interpretation and photographic form.

The Pocket Canons received widespread praise for being a successful update of the Bible. The plaudits are well deserved, but this general assessment is not entirely accurate. More than contemporizing religious texts, these books use archive photography as a means of mapping the Word onto the visually oriented history of the twentieth century. As Umberto Eco has pointed out, "the vicissitudes of [the last] century have been summed up in a few photographs that have been epoch-making."[4] Hyland deliberately avoided the best-known images, but his selection of documentary, still-life, landscape, and portrait photography offers a poetic echo to the more familiar modern picture story. Images remain powerful, of course. But the kind of photographic history that Eco describes ended when new technologies replaced the single epoch-making picture with the indeterminate digital grab. The archive from

the epistle of paul the apostle to the
hebrews

with an introduction by | karen armstrong

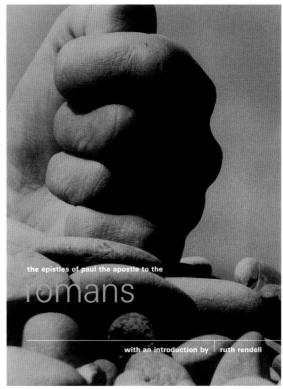

the epistles of paul the apostle to the
romans

with an introduction by | ruth rendell

DREAMER A NOVEL
CHARLES JOHNSON

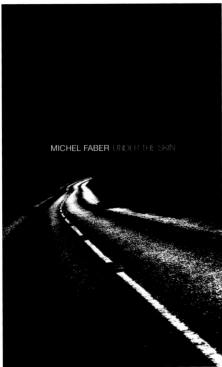

which Hyland drew the biblical covers is already a thing of the past.

Hyland delved back in the twentieth century's photographic holdings for a subsequent Canongate project, the design of the cover for the hardback novel *Dreamer*. Written by Charles Johnson, the book weaves a fiction around the real events in the life of Martin Luther King, and Hyland responded to the work by taking a liberty, albeit a respectful one, with an image of the civil rights martyr. Where most photographs of King are captioned with an estimate of the time between the taking of the picture and the assassination of April 4, 1968, Hyland's cover intimates. coming events in a more direct manner. Piercing a small hole through the paper jacket photograph, he allows the blood red of the book's hard cover to show through King's neck at the entry point of the fatal bullet. With minimal intervention, Hyland turns a photographic image into an illustration of an event. As with the cover of *The Castle*, the effect depends on historical accuracy.

I read *Dreamer* in preparation for this essay. I took it on an airplane, and, being a particularly handsome book, it functioned as a form of readerly self-advertisement. Those around me admired the book, and I believe they were impressed by the apparent worth of its subject. On the way back on the same trip I turned to another of the novels that Hyland has designed for Canongate, Michel Faber's *Under the Skin*. This was a completely different experience. Muffled in an orange jacket with a slightly unpleasant texture, the cover's message is queasily intimate. The Edward Dimsdale photographs of empty roads on the front and back of the book are fairly neutral, but once one is immersed in the story they take on a decidedly sinister tone. I am not going to give away the plot, but reading the book in a single gulp on a transatlantic flight, I often felt the need to tuck the loose cover between the pages to take a breather from its well-paced, stomach-churning revelations. On one of those breaks it struck me that Hyland, who recommended the book highly,

Left: *Covered and uncovered book jacket for Michel Faber's* Under the Skin, *published by Canongate, 2000.*
Opposite: *Book jacket for Charles Johnson's* Dreamer: A Novel, *published by Canongate, 1999.*

With or without feet: a series of talks about type
presented by Creative Review and sponsored by Agfa Monotype

New type design

Pentagram 11 Needham Road London W11 2RP Wednesday 19 February 2003 6.30 PM
tickets £10 students £7.50 email aminah.marshall@centaur.co.uk telephone Gavin Lucas 020 7970 6256
in association with Pentagram Design and Gavin Martin Associates

Typography by hand

Type on screen

must have read it in a completely different form. This might sound naive, but that seemed almost incredible. The book's brooding cover images and its greasy skin seem so much a part of the sensation. Byng told me that, while most foreign publishers insist on their own designs, very few ever tamper with a Hyland creation. The volumes he designs bear the stamp of the definitive.

Among Hyland's most recent projects is a set of posters promoting a series of lectures on typography. Designed before the confirmation of the speakers, these images are less advertisements than discursive pieces in their own right. Up close they look like a grid of red and blue dots; step back and a seminal figure of twentieth-century design appears. This effect is achieved through ASCII art: images built, line by line, from a custom-made 10-dot typeface. These posters represent a sideways move from the historically responsible deployment of pictures that is evident in Hyland's publishing design, toward a broader discussion about the role of photography in the making of history. Concealing the faces of El Lissitzky, Max Bill, and Herbert Bayer in a veil of quasi-typographic information could be seen as going against the grain for a designer known for his typographic restraint. But, far from an uncharacteristic embrace of graphic maximalism, it is a means of making a subtle comment on the group of smartly dressed modernist father figures whose typographic influence continues to hold sway. And, as with all his work, he treats the photographs with utmost propriety. You will never catch Hyland strewing pictures around without care, least of all those of venerable typographers.

1. Peter Wollen, "Fire and Ice," in *Other Than Itself: Writing Photography*, ed. John Berger and Olivier Richon, Manchester: Cornerhouse, 1984.
2. Martha Rosler, "In, Around and Afterthoughts (On Documentary Photography)," in *The Contest of Meaning*, ed. Richard Bolton, Cambridge, MA: MIT Press, 1989.
3. Allan Sekula, "Reading an Archive," in *Photography/Politics Two*, ed. Jo Spence and Simon Watney, London: Comedia, 1986.
4. Umberto Eco, "A Photograph," in *Faith in Fakes*, London: Secker and Warburg, 1986.

Left: Posters designed to promote With or Without Feet, *a series of talks on typography held at Pentagram's offices in London, 2003.*

Three Letters: e.V.O.

Karrie Jacobs on *Paula Scher*

1. WHEN I THINK OF PAULA SCHER, I think of the letter *e*. Lower case. Set in Garamond. A version of the typeface that is faithful to the intentions of its sixteenth-century Parisian designers, Claude Garamond and Jean Jannon.

I identify Paula with this one small but essential vowel because the first time I laid eyes on her she was defending its honor. That was a long time ago, right at the transitional moment when the photocompositor, a method of setting type photographically, with fonts distributed as filmstrips, was yielding to the computer, and fonts were destined to become, along with every other form of information, digital. It was at a time when a lot of intelligent people believed that computers would make type even worse, even more degraded than it had become since the demise of hot, physical metal type. At Type 1987, the conference where I first saw Paula in action, the forward momentum that was driving type further from its solid-lead origins and toward the electronic future engendered a sense of loss. Many of the type designers in attendance seemed to be in a state of mourning.

Not Paula. She was pissed off. At least she came across that way in a debate with Roger Black, the former *Rolling Stone* and *Newsweek* designer. Paula, who was known for her use and creative redeployment of historical typefaces, was incensed that the International Typeface Corporation (ITC), the dominant company in the typositer era, had redrawn their version of the popular typeface Garamond. Black genially defended the company: "ITC's Garamond is a peculiarly contemporary Garamond. It's not a bookish Garamond." But Paula was a firebrand. Like a TV district attorney, she showed her damning evidence, slides of an ITC Garamond *e* and the older Linotype Garamond *e*. She demonstrated that the distinctively high waist of the Garamond *e* had been lowered by ITC and, furthermore, that they had fiddled with the lowercase *a*, plumping it a bit. "The problem with the new form is it's called Garamond and it's not Garamond," Paula declaimed. "I'd like them to take it back, admit it..." At that moment, Paula was my hero. While her

Opposite: Poster for the Public Theater's production of Fucking A, *a play by Suzan-Lori Parks, 2003.*

complaints about the typeface focused on details that would be trivial to anyone who was not of the rarefied breed I later came to think of as the "type-head," they actually touched on issues that were major, such as the commodification of culture and the corruption of creative ideas through mass marketing. These were big-ticket issues. It felt like Paula, by taking on ITC, was getting at what was wrong with things that were more central than lowercase letters. Of course, if you really think about it, nothing is more central than lowercase letters.

"Oh yeah. Oh yeah," she now recalls, "ITC was an absolute enemy to me. They were just so dominant in the phototypositer era that their faces erased the existence of more authentic faces." As it turns out, the computer saved the day when a whole new type

industry grew up around it. "It wasn't until Adobe Garamond that the actual, better-drawn Garamond came back," she says, acknowledging the contributions of a pioneering electronic-type company.

While the small, close-knit society of type designers is full of people who endlessly lament the current state of the art—whatever that state happens to be—Paula's argument was compelling because it seemed driven not by fear of the new but by a powerful connection to the letterforms themselves. She viewed them not as an antiquarian might but rather as someone who used letters—old, forgotten,

Above and opposite: Painted exterior of the Lucent Technologies Center for Arts Education, a school affiliated with the New Jersey Performing Arts Center in Newark, 2001.

obsolete letters—in a hands-on way. She had an unusual intimacy with the letterforms because she entered the design profession as a renegade, rejecting the available typographic tools to make her own.

Back in art school in Philadelphia, Paula had decided to become an illustrator, but the only way to study illustration there was to take the graphic-design program. "You couldn't just do the illustration," she explains. "You had to do the illustration and type. And the technology at the time was press-type. Everybody went out and bought Helvetica and they rubbed it down in the corner.

"We had all learned graphic design as the Swiss international system," she continues. "It was Helvetica on the grid, very much like what stuff looks like now, very clean, very anal, and completely anti my view of being an artist, which was much more expressive than that. It seemed to be some kind of thing my mother devised to keep the house neat. So I'd do whatever it was, a record cover, a book jacket, what have you, and I'd buy some terrible typeface and rub the press-type down badly in the corner and the thing would break and crackle and it would always look like crap."

Her teacher Stanislaw Zagorski finally clued her in to an alternative: "'Illustrate the type,'" she remembers him saying. "'Look at the type as illustration.' And it dawned on me that the stuff had form."

Paula began drawing type and immersed herself in its architecture. At her first real job, as an art director at CBS Records, she began, over time, to design record covers that were purely typographic. The typefaces she'd use were borrowed from motley sources. An expert scavenger, she would lift a cartoony font from an antique pipe-tobacco canister or dig up historical wooden type at the Morgan Library. Paula had cultivated a relationship with type as an artifact, a physical piece of design with its own history and culture, like a McCoy vase or a Thonet chair.

2. When I think of Paula Scher, I think of the letter V, a boldfaced uppercase letter so sturdy as to appear three-dimensional, one that dominates its sheet of paper as powerfully as a Richard Serra

Left: Environmental graphics for Symphony Space, a community arts center on Manhattan's Upper West Side, 2002.

sculpture dominates a plaza. This *V* is the focal point, the sun that holds all the other elements in their orbits, on a poster Paula designed for the Public Theater for the 1996 Shakespeare Festival in Central Park.

I regard this poster, a big rectangle in gradated shades of orange and yellow announcing the plays *Henry V* and *Timon of Athens*, as a treatise on Paula's relationship with type. The letterforms are all thick and solid. They look powerfully contemporary, but, like many of the album covers Paula designed in the 1970s, they are composed of old wooden type. The difference is that while the type in the '70s posters is all dolled up in the stylistic affectations of the time—drop shadows and sweet Victorian colors—the letterforms in this poster are stripped down to the essentials.

"You might be disappointed in the answer," Paula says, trying to tell me that the poster is not her declaration of love for that monumental hunk of type. No, she insists, it's something perfectly reasoned and dispassionate. "There's a specific problem, and the problem is that you have two unrelated plays and one of them has a real long title and the other doesn't. Poster design has to function with some sort of strong focal point, or it all has to be texture. It's really a design principle. If you can make that *V* as big as possible it's going to hold all this related stuff together. So that this is all scale and balanced decision making, which is what one does with typography."

Fine. Maybe it is all diligent, responsible, creative problem solving, a professional just doing what she's got to do. But the Public Theater posters that Paula has been turning out since 1994 look to me like a release valve for untold quantities of pent-up typographic steam. They start out in the '94 season with big, bold type, pretty loud, but there's still some breathing room between words. The next season she begins to fiddle with the type in ways that recall her early album covers. For instance, in a poster for a play about the Venus Hottentot she turns an outsized capital *U* into the underpinning for the central character's most remarkable physical feature, more evidence that, for Paula, type is not two-dimensional, a series of skinny lines, but something physical, something with mass and heft.

This typographic showmanship, however, is just a warm-up for subsequent efforts in which the intensity and density of the type on Paula's posters for the Public appear to max out the ink-bearing capacity of the paper. Paula is displaying, perhaps for the first time, the unbridled power of her obsession with type. Her professional output is offering a clue about who she truly is. These posters are the confession of a typographic obsessive.

3. When I think of Paula Scher, I think of a hand-painted capital *O*, all goony and distended, like one of those homemade cider donuts they sell at the farmers' market. This *O* is just one of hundreds of thousands of letters, some in white with red borders and others in yellow, with soft, buttery edges. All of them are crowded together, with no room to breathe. Letters on top of letters on top of letters.

Paula, as it turns out, is not in her heart of hearts a graphic designer, even though she has been successfully posing as one her whole adult life. Rather, she is an outsider artist, as crazed about typography as the Reverend Howard Finster was about his garden of spiritually driven sculpture. She is to the canvas as Dr. Bronner is to the soap bottle. She approaches the world like Nagiko, heroine of Peter Greenaway's movie *The Pillow Book*, who viewed each new lover as a slate for her calligraphy. Left to her own devices, there is no limit to how much type Paula will squeeze onto a surface. Left to her own devices, there is hardly a surface Paula would leave unlettered. I ask her an innocent question: "What else would you put type on if they let you?" "Everything," she replies. "I'd put type on everything. I'd put it on the streets, everywhere. I'd love to be the art director of New York City. I'd plaster the place with it."

Actually, she is being asked more and more often to cover buildings with letters. In Newark, she painted a high school for the performing arts white, like a crisp, unblemished sheet of paper, and then put words like "theater," "dance," and "poetry" in stylish outline capital letters all over it. In the spirit of 1970s supergraphics, Paula has run giant words down the halls and up the walls of the 42nd Street Studios building. Currently she's working with Pentagram partner Lisa Strausfeld to incorporate electronic type throughout the new Bloomberg News building next door to Bloomingdale's. One by one, building by building,

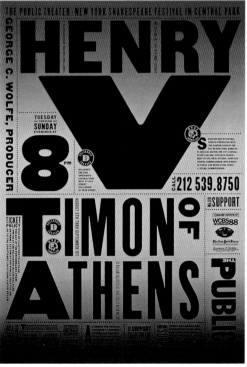

Paula is becoming the art director of New York. But it's not enough. It's never enough.

In her spare time, in the country house in Connecticut that she shares with her husband, the illustrator Seymour Chwast, she paints maps of the United States and maps of the world with the names of places lettered in layers and layers, large town names over small town names and state names over city names. These maps are the antithesis of the Helvetica and grid design that she initially rejected back in art school. There is no system here, no grid, and not a lick of white space. The very idea of white space does not exist in the world as mapped by Paula. Nor is there room for the dark matter that physicists theorize constitutes 99 percent of the universe, not in the universe as painted by Paula.

If the Public Theater posters, brash and exuberant, seem like a natural outgrowth of all the design gestures that Paula has made in her career, all her thoughts about the formal qualities of type and the ways you can use antique type in extremely contemporary ways, if the Public Theater posters are a primal blast of professional acuity and confidence, the maps are a private, almost antiprofessional response to thirty years of practice. They are her grandest insurrection.

The hand-painted maps are Paula's response to two irritants in the life of a graphic designer: the tyranny of the computer and the ubiquity of the client.

"I love the labor of painting the typography," Paula explains. "I used to do record covers before there was computing. I used to sit in my office at CBS Records with a phone in my ear, talking to a manager, painting type on an overlay of some bad photo of a recording artist. It was very satisfying to have the ability to actually touch art supplies. The computer took all that away from me. It took away my hands to a degree. So the idea of doing this laborious kind of word painting is a little bit about what I feel like I lost in terms of my craft.

"But the other part is that I like the idea of controlling my own information," she continues. "If I design a poster or a building or a magazine, I don't

Top left: Poster for the New York Shakespeare Festival's 2003 production of Henry V. *Left: Poster for the festival's 1996 season of* Henry V *and* Timon of Athens.

get to write the copy. I'm told that things have to go there. I'm chastised if something is misspelled. Things have to be in the right spot. I make a map and people walk up to the map and say, 'Oh, I've been there,' and they point to a place and it's absolutely in the wrong spot. I just think that's a hoot. It's useless information," she adds. "It's completely useless information, but at least I'm in control of it, and I think it's as good as anybody else's useless information."

So we've established that Paula Scher is an obsessive typographer, spending her workday applying type to any surface that she can get her hands on and occupying herself on weekends painting letters on canvas. But is there a limit? Is there *anything* that Paula wouldn't put type on? "Good question," she says. "I haven't thought about it." She struggles to come up with an answer. She likes type on people, thinks tattoos are great, enjoys graffiti, appreciates almost all forms of signage, including commercial billboards and roadside neon letters that say "EAT." Finally, after an uncharacteristically long pause, she comes up with the one thing that she doesn't want to art-direct: "I don't want to put type on my dog."

Left: Africa, *one of Scher's personal paintings, acrylic on canvas, 9 x 10 feet, 2003.*

The Modest Art of Design

Deyan Sudjic on *Daniel Weil*

RAYMOND LOEWY, MASTER OF SELF-PUBLICITY and the Lucky Strike packet, continues to cast a long shadow over the practice of design. Loewy invented the idea of the designer as heroic form giver, destined to don a white suit and play the magician, picking inspiration out of thin air. And this is still the model—give or take a few Calvinist exceptions—for the aspiring designer in the English- and French-speaking worlds, even for those not blessed with Loewy's shameless silver-tongued eloquence. The kind of designer ready to declaim that what the client really needs is Yves Klein Blue. Or to say that the client, even though he doesn't know it, can't manage without a radio shaped to look like a trumpet, or a shop that evokes the fashion sense of the German Democratic Republic. This is the kind of designer who cannot be stopped from telling the world that his wretched sofa is designed to suggest the act of making love. We know perfectly well that it is an antediluvian conception of design. We tell ourselves that we no longer believe in it as a template, or in the tyranny of the object for that matter. Except, of course, that we do. Confront even the most skeptical of us with a seductive piece of consumer electronics aimed at the early adopter, and we are ready to roll over and play dead for a tickle from any of the procession of latter-day would-be Loewys.

There are of, course, rather more sophisticated ideas of what design can be. When Daniel Weil was a student in London in the 1970s, the Loewy tendency was, temporarily as it turned out, moribund. Weil and his generation were clear that design had a cultural significance deeper than streamlining the sales curve. They were more interested in the idea of systems and methodology than in showmanship. Weil was intrigued in particular by the idea of design as a language. Weil brought with him from his native Argentina an architectural education, a well-developed interest in Marcel Duchamp, and a copy of Noam Chomsky. It is a combination that has shaped his work and his attitudes to design in an attempt to combine the personal with the universal. In particular, he has always tried to look beyond

Opposite: Cutlery for United Airlines, part of a design program that includes airplane interiors, all on-board products, airport self-service check-in facilities, and lounges, 1999–present.

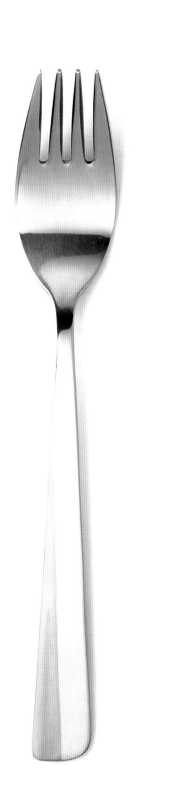

the obvious, to understand that the answer to a designer's brief may not actually be an object at all. At a moment when for some designers a commission from a mobile-telephone company interested in communicating its new-generation technology to potential customers is taken as a license to design a shop, that is a more radical stance than it might sound. Like the avid student of philosophy that he was, Weil never leaves the a priori—such as the actual needs for "objects"—uninterrogated. This is an intellectual who has devoted himself to what is often the least introspective and least self-effacing of professions: design.

Designers now operate in a climate in which any conversation with an airline is understood as an invitation to repaint every aircraft in its fleet and stencil a new logo on the tails. And those who do talk about strategy tend to do so in the abstract rather than use it as the starting point for design. It is perfectly possible to operate as a designer at this level. But to do so is to miss the point. Design in this sense becomes a kind of cargo cult, a matter of going through the formal motions that appear to deliver the goods rather than actually making them. Like the isolated South Sea islanders who believed that all that was necessary to achieve the return of the first contact ship (and more of the industrial goods that it had brought with it that they craved) was to form a welcoming committee to greet it, they deliver strategy without substance, advice without evidence. And those designers who take their clients' wishes at face value, designing shops because that is what designers design, miss the point that the real answer to the brief might be something quite different. The point of the exercise is, well, sometimes you don't know exactly what it is until you have, as Weil puts it, made some connections. Few designers have pursued a career path that has more closely mirrored the shifts in the practice of design than Daniel Weil, whose work has ranged from handmade transistor radios in customized bags to large-scale commercial interiors. He has moved from outsider to insider. He has worked on his own and as part of a large team. He has made one-offs and designed mass-produced objects. He has used design as a means of cultural expression and a commercial weapon.

It's not that Weil is uninterested in the tactile and physical qualities of design. But that is just one aspect of it. Weil's view of design is of a complex territory that can be read on several different levels. His pre-Pentagram career saw him using design as the starting point for a series of musings on the nature of things and their significance. In the decade he has been at Pentagram, he has put to work the conceptual tools developed during his years as a designer who was largely his own client to a more conventional working context. But Weil sees no contradictions between the two approaches. His work can be understood on different levels and is aimed simultaneously at very different people, for managers as well as their customers, and/or the employees who serve them. It is designed to make commercial sense as well as to have cultural integrity and meaning in his personal voyage of discovery through the world of design. And if this sounds like an attempt at having it both ways, well, yes, it is. As Weil says, "All designers must have as their objective to be artists. But art is defined by context. Your personal experience does not make it art."

And that is why Weil measures out his work not as a series of individual episodes but as a continuous process. He believes "design is about careers and not the moment. It's not one wonderful piece, it's a trajectory." That is why Weil is ready to see his career as moving through different phases, some more commercial than art. But a commercial view of design was not his starting point. It is much harder, he thinks, to do things the other way around. "Start commercial, and you tend to end up commercial." For Weil, "the role of the designer is to connect the commercial and art." Weil does design discrete interiors. He has designed objects, though recently they are as likely to take the form of the packaging as of their contents. But they tend to be in the context of a wider relationship with a client, and they often involve other Pentagram partners, John Rushworth and Michael Bierut in particular.

United Airlines is a case in point. Pentagram's relationship with the carrier has been a protracted one, which over the years has outlasted successive management teams that have come and gone and a shifting series of objectives, from the creation of one

of the first airline identities of the new age of global network alliances to the challenge of no-frills budget airlines. In the process, the Pentagram team has become what amounts to the company's memory. "As a designer you have a different type of clarity from your client's clarity. You try to connect different parts of the organization." What Weil worked on was to create a sense of what United needed to be as an airline and to make each individual piece of the project for the company reflect that sense. But it was a process that went beyond how things looked: It depended also on understanding the increasingly sophisticated tastes of the business-class passenger,

Above: Headrest, pillows, blankets, mattress and seat fabric for United First Suite, part of the full airplane-interior decor program for United Airlines, 1999–present.

the way that the cabin staff serve them food, and the nature of the purchasing process that supplies the airline. In short, Weil analyzed the culture of flying and the culture of food. "United's crockery used to include grey burgundy-colored trim that made the food look bad. They looked as if they came from the kind of restaurant that somebody's grandfather used to go to. We wanted to incorporate a more modern expectation."

But even more important for Pentagram was to understand how its client worked and just who it was that was responsible for buying the crockery. It was not a board-level decision, yet it was one that would have a direct impact on every passenger on every flight. "Any large organization is only as good as its component parts; you have to reverse the pyramid and put the most sophisticated people at

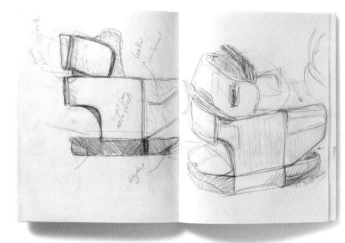

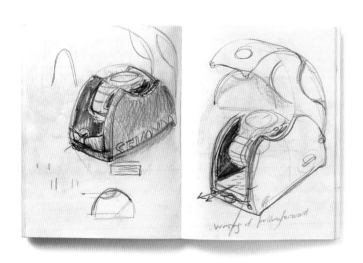

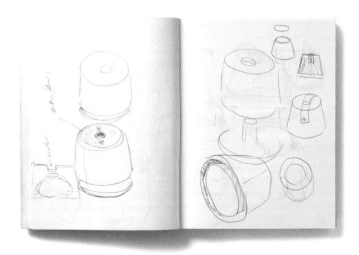

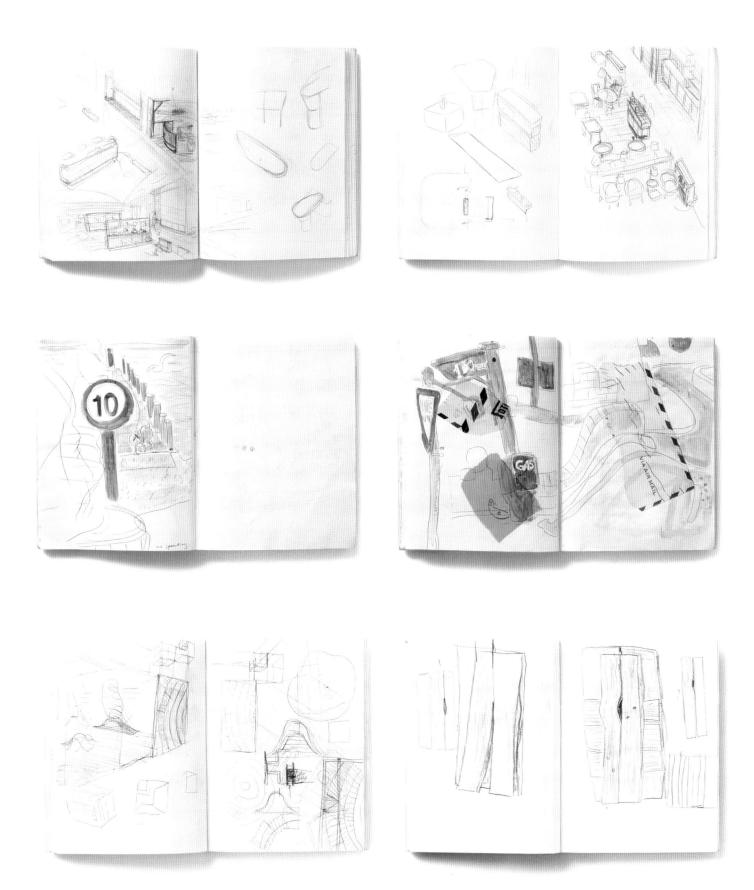

the base." Weil challenged United to move beyond the personal choice of the individual, to establish the grounds for making a more rational choice. "The first issue was the customer experience, the second was the food quality, and the third was to come up with different options for the same items for the same price. If you succeed in understanding the purchasing process, then you can succeed in making it cheaper as well as better." In the end Weil devised a plain white plate with no United logo, in a quiet rebuke to the obsessive tendency of big corporations to cover their products in the most obvious forms of branding.

Weil and his team have had to deal with every one of a hundred other objects for United in the same level of painstaking detail, from the blankets handed out in the cabin to the fabric on the seats to the luggage label. At each stage he has seen it as just as important to make clear how each decision has been made, to create a climate in which the organization itself can learn how to do things in the same way. "I like making sense of things and making the process transparent. It's not about being systematic but about revealing your tricks. Design is not methodology: Every project requires different stacking and different degrees of softness and rigidity. Design is about thinking, but thinking becomes very visual for me."

Weil's most powerful personal working tool remains the drawing. He covers roll after roll of paper with his elegant, limpid pencil-and-ink sketches. He fills them out from left to right in a continually unraveling band, like the Bayeux tapestry. They dart from subject to subject, rather like his conversation, a reflection of a mind always looking for connections. And like his conversation, his drawings sometimes pause in midflow to elaborate a theme or an issue at a deeper level, in the shape of an exquisitely finished watercolor. The results are transformed into the reports he writes for clients, illustrated by storyboards and mood illustrations. But it is his drawings that are fundamental to his work.

Previous spread: Weil's open sketchbooks. **Left:** *Retail interiors for the mobile-telephone company Quam, Germany, 2002.* **Opposite:** *Interiors for A Cafe, Italy, 2000.*

You can trace out the intellectual underpinning to his designs for Quam, a third-generation mobile-telephone company in Germany, in those drawings. Quam no longer exists, the victim of the fast-changing market. It was bought up and shut down by a rival network, but it demonstrated Weil's attitudes to the design process. It was a start-up company that had to communicate what it could offer to potential customers. For Weil that was the point of departure for an exploration of the significance of the mobile phone. Rather than understanding the new-generation technology as concerned primarily with mobility, he saw G3 phones, which offer limitless roaming potential, as having the possibility of making domesticity possible everywhere. "That was the big connective idea: domesticity. The home is the center of everything; in fact, home is a minimodel of the city." It was an insight that could be applied to the products Quam offered, as well as the way it sold them. Why not, Weil asked, use the power of G3 to offer customers a personal digital attic, to store all

that information that gets lost when you leave it in a telephone memory or a hard drive or a digital camera? "You can just send it all away and access it any time you need it. It is a very domestic idea. It's a personal digital attic." The same domestic metaphor of the house informed the nature of the network of shops that Weil designed for Quam. "The idea was to offer the reassurance of the familiar."

The Goodwood gallery in London is a project that allowed Weil to work on a very different scale. The Goodwood trust is a charity established to promote British sculpture. Weil has worked with the Cass family to design the gallery and to convert an adjacent property into Focus, a linked photographic gallery. There are two distinct but linked spaces. One has a little more domestic flavor, a personal, private space with a small indoor garden lit by glass bricks. The other is darker and more theatrical with a big double void. Here Weil has had the space to work on what is primarily an architectural project. His methods have been applied not to an organization but, with equal power, to an architectural hierarchy, suggesting that he is a designer whose trajectory is indeed directed at art rather than commerce.

Below: Watch packaging for Sekonda, 2003. **Opposite:** *Front door for the Sculpture at Goodwood gallery, London, 2003.*

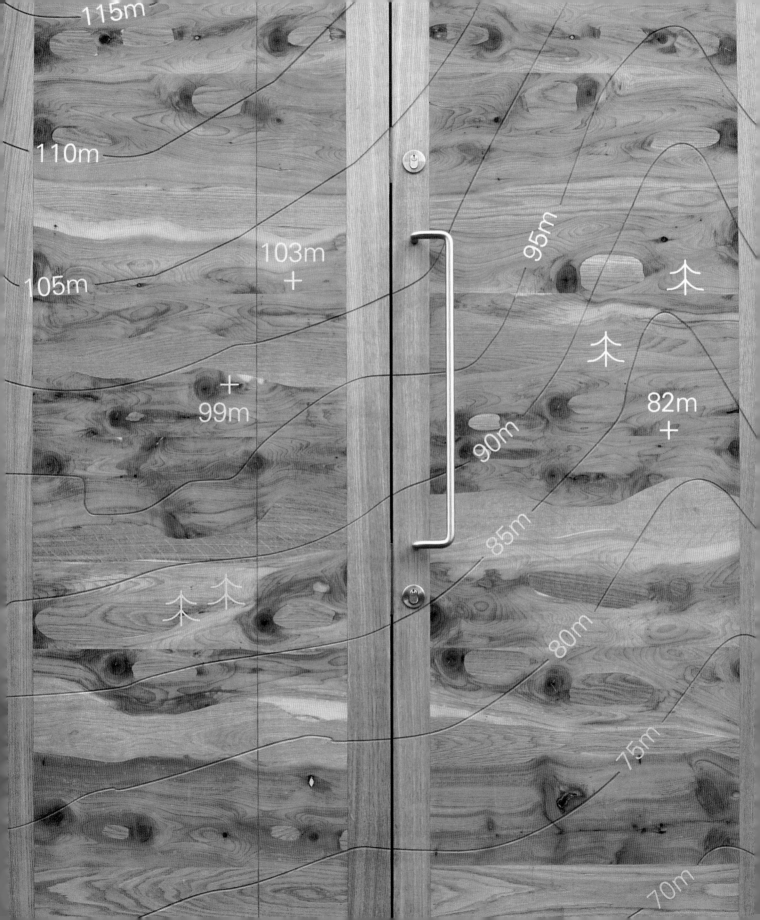

All-American

Kurt Andersen on *Michael Bierut*

I AM UNABLE TO WRITE OBJECTIVELY about Michael Bierut. The conflicts of interest are vast. When in 1994 I became editor of *New York* magazine and needed someone to refurbish the logo, I hired Pentagram. Michael's response to that huge, juicy opportunity was to present me with two options: a wholly new sans serif logo and a tweaked version of Peter Palazzo's original logo for the magazine from the days when it was an insert in the Sunday *New York Herald Tribune*. ("Palazzo's logo with a haircut," he called it at the time.) And incredibly, it was the latter solution—respectful, conservative in the best sense— that he pushed. I agreed, and we became friends. And when I helped start Inside.com a few years later, I turned to Michael again. He and his colleagues engineered the perfect Inside logo and Web site format and then, incredibly, in less than two months, helped us design the biweekly *Inside* magazine from scratch. Finally, and most incredibly of all, even though I stiffed him on his fee for that last project, we remained friends.

I think the key to understanding Michael Bierut's work is the quintessential Americanism of his temperament. We can all point to plenty of lousy design that also happens to be quintessentially American: most packages on the shelves of most stores, most new houses, most cars. But when I look at the body of Michael's work—and for that matter, at Michael himself—the common threads I see are most of the admirable American virtues. By which I mean, not to put too fine a point on it, the virtues embodied by (for instance) Benjamin Franklin and Mark Twain and Charles and Ray Eames: industry, populism, pragmatism, playfulness, honesty, unpretentiousness, a sense of humor, a light touch, an appreciation of pleasure, a basic frugality, a rejection of cant, a cheerful magpie mongrelism, a balance between city-on-a-hill conviction and big-tent laissez-faire tolerance.

Consider, for starters, his deeply and unglamorously all-American boyhood. He grew up Roman Catholic in Parma, Ohio, a suburb of Cleveland that makes Cleveland look cosmopolitan. His father was a Polish-American printing-press salesman.

Opposite: "Game Face" mascot from an identity program for the New York Jets, 2001.

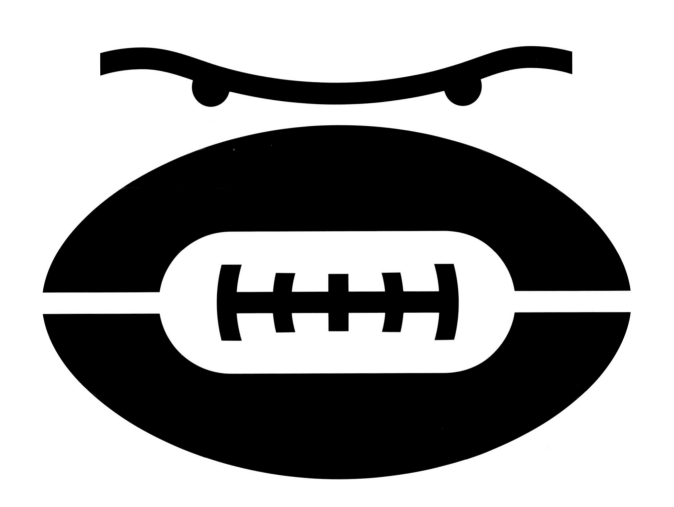

NEW YORK

[INSIDE]

He attended a high school that had, as he puts it, "a vocational/technical bent." And from these authentically humble beginnings he discovered his calling early on, like the kid who knows he wants to enter the priesthood—but in his case, to become a priest of the aesthetic religion of no-religion.

As a teenager in the uncoolest precincts of flyover-land, he discovered he could draw well, then stumbled across the exotic profession of graphic design and, *boom*, knew with the certainty of revelation that that's what he wanted to be. His DIY catechism consisted of three books: *Aim for a Job in Graphic Design*, which happened to be in his high school guidance office; a Basel design manual that was, improbably, in the stacks of his local public library; and Milton Glaser's brand-new *Graphic Design*, which his parents bought for him. In other words, straightforward practicality, European modernist rigor, and virtuosic American pop eclecticism. "From the beginning, I had a mixed religious background, high and populist."

After the University of Cincinnati, he came straight to New York to work for Massimo Vignelli, maybe the last, best high-modernist graphic designer in America. And he produced impeccable Vignelli-esque work—lucid, crisp, relentlessly clean, seriously handsome. "I'm an excellent mimic," he says of his successful run there, which is characteristically self-deprecating as well as true. So while he was a skillful and eager apprentice for a decade and became a Vignelli favorite, he is not in his gut a disciple, was never a po-faced true believer in the fundamental and unquestionable superiority of Helvetica over Franklin Gothic or Bodoni over Century Schoolbook. In other words, even as an impressionable young man he was skeptical, non-doctrinaire, antidogmatic. It is American to believe in fundamentals with unbudging passion only when there are fundamental principles involved; choice of typeface simply never rises to that level. In the Bierutian view, Vignelli's high modernism was *a* style but never *the* style.

Nor, fortunately for Michael, was Vignelli himself really a control-freak purist—he is Italian,

Top left: Redeveloped logotype for New York *magazine, 1994.*
Left: Identity for media journal Inside.com, 2000.

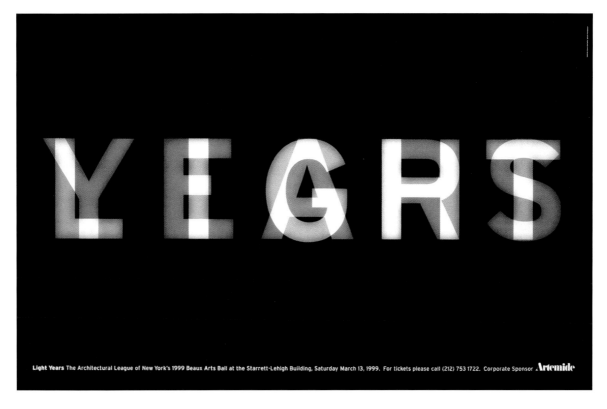

Light Years The Architectural League of New York's 1999 Beaux Arts Ball at the Starrett-Lehigh Building, Saturday March 13, 1999. For tickets please call (212) 753 1722. Corporate Sponsor .Artemide

after all, not actually Swiss. "In his Italianate way," his former colleague recalls, "Massimo loved the occasional emotional personal gesture." For Michael, the little breakthrough "personal gesture" came in a piece of work in the 1980s for IDCNY, the International Design Center of New York, whose strictly Bodoni-driven graphic identity he had already created with Vignelli. IDCNY needed invitations for two events, one celebrating NASA designers and one celebrating Memphis design. The budget allowed only for a single, combined invitation for these two entirely disparate parties. But Michael— pragmatic, hands-on, good-humored, ad hoc, economical, unflappably American Michael— roughed out a sketch that killed both birds with one stone: He found that the nose cone and fins of an upside-down rocket resembled… a Memphis table, and, of course, vice versa. Problem solved. His cartoony, schoolboyish doodle became

Above: Poster for the Architectural League of New York's annual beaux-arts gala, 1999.

the centerpiece of the consolidated invitation; lemons into lemonade.

It was postmodern—decorative, handcrafted, winking—but postmodernism very lightly worn, with none of the show-offy hoo-ha that so often characterizes artifacts of an up-and-coming Movement. Michael Bierut came of age at a moment in design history that suited his essentially eclectic, fun-loving—i.e., American—temperament. With the regime change accomplished by postmodernism, which occurred just as he graduated from design school, mutts ruled. Fun was privileged. But Michael was no po-mo ideologue of the antimodernist stripe. He was not driven to kill his professional father but rather to declare himself the adopted son, stylistically and conceptually, of multiple fathers and mothers. His apostasy was not to reject one paradigmatic tyranny in favor of a new one but to embrace and epitomize a sort of design libertarianism. Let a hundred flowers bloom—including flowers from Basel. This is the sense in which he is the good kind of conservative, not a reactionary: Instead of

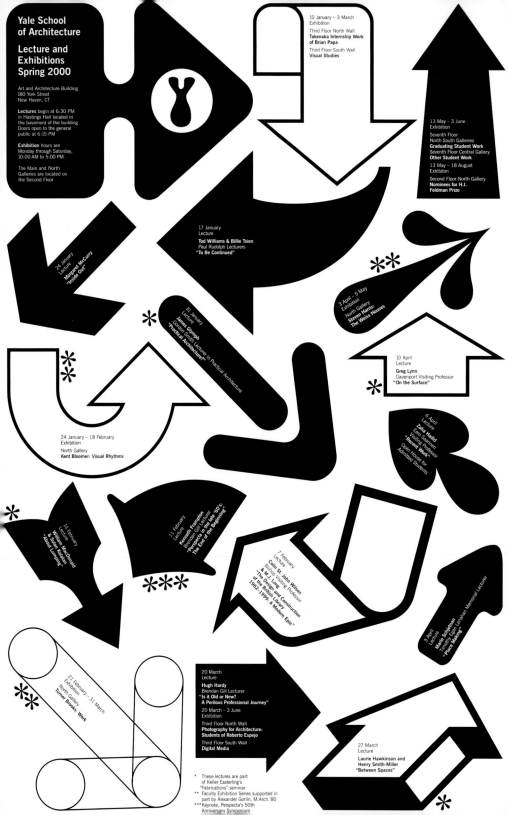

fetishizing the old and the canonical, he regards established styles as a trove from which he can pick and choose at will. He was raised Catholic, but as a designer he is, instead, catholic. Thus he arrived at Pentagram, going "from monotheism to pantheism, which suited me more."

One still sees in Michael's work to this day some of the gestures and lessons—lucidity, rigor, Bodoni—that were baked into his brain at the seminary of Saint Massimo. When he designed new graphics for the refurbished Lever House on Park Avenue a few years ago, for instance, he did what he'd done for me at *New York*, but more elaborately: He took the eight sans serif letterforms from a Lever House sign that had been designed for the building in 1952—*L, E, V, R, H, O, U,* and *S*—and from those commissioned a full-alphabet font called Lever Sans. The result is signage that looks like it was always there. "It's less about nostalgia," he says, "than about self-effacement, to not intrude, to build on the familiar." On the other hand, there are times when teasing out the existing institutional DNA is not possible, or desirable. As an architect Robert A. M. Stern is a nostalgia monger and has even been an historicist ideologue, but as the dean of the Yale School of Architecture for the last five years he has sought, sensibly, to impose no monolithic house style. So he hired Michael to design highly eclectic formats for the school's communications—posters, a newsletter, the whole shebang. The riot of typefaces and visual layering sends the unequivocal message that New Haven is now multidenominational.

It is not only highfalutin stylistic doctrines of which Michael steers clear. In 2000, a group of graphic designers published an anticonsumerist jeremiad called the "First Things First Manifesto" that exhorted designers to do work that promotes (not-for-profit) culture and (lefty) social and political messages rather than consumer products. Michael is no philistine nor, as far as I know, a Republican. But if he were not hardwired to be so cheerful he would be a curmudgeon. The critique he published of the "First Things First Manifesto" was withering.

Left: Environmental graphics for the renovated Lever House, New York, 2002. **Opposite:** *Poster for the Yale School of Architecture, 1999.*

"What makes dog biscuit packaging an unworthy object of our attention," he wondered, "as opposed to, say, a Walker Art Center catalog? Don't dachshund owners deserve some measure of beauty, wit and intelligence in their lives, too.... Manifestoes are simple; life is complicated." And as he said to me recently, "I think of design not as something that's supposed to startle people into changing their lives, but to elevate their everyday lives."

Which isn't to say he's oblivious to the dangers of consumer-culture glibness. Take the artificially sweet town of Celebration, Disney's New Urbanist Lite development outside Orlando. When Disney hired him to confect their confected town's signage, he invented a fictional backstory involving a local sign painter who produced the simple, pseudo-vernacular street signs. But Disney, of course, also wanted a logo for the town. "We said, 'Towns have seals, not "logos." Real people have actually got to live here.'" In fact, the seal looks a lot like a logo to me—a silhouette of girl riding a bike with a dog running after her. But it is evocative, if just this side of treacly, and nails the good-old-fashioned Americana that Celebration—and, indeed, New Urbanism generally—is about. Yet in this connection Michael frets, at least a little, about the ultrafluency and promiscuity inherent in his profession. "Where I have qualms is how easily graphic designers go in and hit the note. As opposed to architects, who have to be such believers."

Of course, if a designer doesn't subscribe to an all-defining Big Idea and have a more or less all-purpose signature template into which every project can be squeezed, he is making life more difficult for himself. He can become a hack, like most people in any nominally creative profession, providing clients with likable, easy, familiar solutions. Or else he must think and sweat every time out, trying to divine some fresh way to solve the problem at hand. He has to come up with an idea.

Like all of the great graphic designers with whom I've had the good fortune to work over the years,

*Top left: The Fashion Center Information Kiosk in New York's garment district, 1996. **Left:** Environmental graphics for the town of Celebration, Florida, 1995. **Opposite:** Illustrations for the op-ed page of the* New York Times, *1997–2003.*

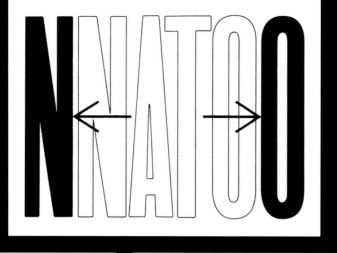

Michael is engaged in the wider world of ideas and information as well as fonts and paper stocks and Pantone colors. He is a reader and a thinker. His gift is the ability to transmute complicated thoughts into rich, economical images. His occasional *New York Times* op-ed pieces are among the clearest examples of this knack for distillation. A few years ago, when a generation of political liberals found themselves for the first time in favor of US military intervention, in Kosovo, he rendered the phrase "Give War A Chance" in classic psychedelic-poster letterforms. To illustrate the case against bringing countries of the former Soviet empire into NATO, he simply doubled and boldfaced the first and last letters of the acronym to express the idea of NO. Similarly, his identity program for New York's new Museum of Sex was as elegant as could be: a bold-face *X* at the end of the key word, and similar understated *X* shapes on signage throughout the building. In other words, he seems always to seek ways to be appropriately playful whenever playfulness is remotely appropriate.

Michael seems to do some of his most inspired work as a celebrant of New York City. A decade ago, the Fashion Center Business Improvement District asked him to "re-dress" an information kiosk on Seventh Avenue at Thirty-ninth Street. His simple, grand, delightfully Oldenburgian solution, executed with his partner, James Biber, was to replace it entirely with a giant steel sewing needle, a giant fiberglass button, and a giant spool of thread. A few miles south is the smartest street signage in town, also his doing, in this instance for the Alliance for Downtown New York. The actual street signs are smart because they assume pedestrian ignorance: The sign on each corner gives the range of address numbers on that block. And the information kiosks for tourists are smart because they don't strain to seem smart: Instead of inventing, say, an abstracted graphic symbol for the Chrysler Building or the Seaport, the kiosks simply reproduce photographs of the buildings in question. "As an older designer," Michael says, "I'm more willing to be dumb and straightforward." Given the assignment of redesign-

ing the New York Jets' graphics, he was both Respectful Michael and Playful Michael. (And also Charmingly But Somewhat Disingenuously Self-Deprecating Michael: "I don't know football, so I did what I always do—I ordered two books from Amazon and crammed for a weekend.") For his raw material he used—like he did with the midcentury swank of Lever House—the Jets' existing logo from the early '60s. From the four letters in "Jets" he propagated a whole new font (Jets Bold) and then rendered it jauntily, as he says, "to *look* like a *chant*." And from the iconic football on the old logo his design team reconstituted the lacing into a kind of graphic-design mascot for the team—a funny-scary Homer Simpson-esque grimace called "Game Face."

He may not care about football, but he is, I think, as much a team player as anyone I've ever met. These days, whom else do you know in their forties who has worked for only two companies? He's that rare person of real talent to whom collegiality comes at least as naturally as egomania. He seems to enjoy collaboration rather than merely tolerate it. And as far as I can tell, his menschy affect is natural and guileless—that is, utterly undesigned.

Opposite: Streetscape signage program for Lower Manhattan, 2000.

Sensuality at Scale

Jeremy Myerson on *Lorenzo Apicella*

THERE IS ONE QUESTION that Lorenzo Apicella has faced all his professional life. So when it was raised during discussions in the run-up to his joining Pentagram as a partner, the Italian-born Renaissance man knew exactly what to say. To the inquiry "Would you call yourself a designer or an architect?" he replied, "I'm a designer who makes buildings."

In one succinct statement, he articulated a design ethos that would resonate within the multi-disciplinary community of Pentagram. Here was an architect describing a holistic approach to design and a belief in the craft of making buildings work. Here was a view of architecture not as the domineering mother of the arts, monolithic and frozen in time, but as a branch of design, as a form of communication, as a spectacle or event that people experience for a duration.

When Lorenzo Apicella became a partner in 1998, he brought into Pentagram a wide-ranging portfolio. His projects, spanning from mobile exhibitions and delicate studio interiors to conceptual master plans and giant office towers, expressed an idea of central importance: that making buildings is an activity akin to stagecraft, an activity capable of—indeed, ideally suited to—the imperatives of a newly emerging "experience economy."

Even as an architectural student in the late 1970s, Apicella had been drawn to architecture as an event or experience for people as much as a formal academic discipline. Tellingly, at Canterbury School of Art he chose as the subject of his dissertation the life and work of a relatively obscure eighteenth-century French architect called Jean-Jacques Lequeu whose career was cut short by the French Revolution.

Due to the politics of the age, Lequeu was not able to realize many of his buildings but he was prolific on paper and as a set designer and painter, creating "street" architecture and events. Apicella was clearly inspired by Lequeu's ability to deal with architecture on several different scales, from transient structure to city plan. The Frenchman's approach, described by one architectural historian as a sequence of strange and wonderful things, would resonate in Apicella's project work over the next

Opposite: Detail of Clear Channel International Building, London, 2003.

twenty years, in its mix of the temporary and the permanent, in the sheer variety of ways it responded to the dictates of site and brief.

What would the Pentagram partners make of Apicella's practice? Architecture had not always sat entirely comfortably within the Pentagram firmament. On one famous occasion in the early days of the firm in London, Bob Gill leaned over Theo Crosby's shoulder while he was working on plans for a shopping center and asked when it would be finished. "In seven years," replied Crosby. "That's a long time to wait for a proof," sniffed Gill.

But Lorenzo Apicella's work seemed tailor-made to fill a notoriously difficult berth. It evidently owed as much to the cut and thrust of contemporary design, with its short deadlines, brand messages, and business imperatives, as it did to the philosophical traditions of architectural practice.

All his techno-futuristic trade stands, lightweight, collapsible structures, colorful restaurants, and trademark towers demonstrated the work of a natural communicator as well as a thoughtful designer. Here was an architecture of communication. Building as billboard. Environment as event. Setting as spectacle.

If the fit was perfect for Pentagram, it was because Apicella's career was well tailored. The first perspective to imprint itself on him was acquired in the office of the London architect Michael Mitchell, a Miesian disciple who applied himself to all the design disciplines, including graphics, furniture, and lighting. The experience he acquired there was refined in the Houston office of the US firm Skidmore, Owings & Merrill (SOM), where he was entrusted to work on the seventy-story Allied Bank Plaza Building. These two stints in major professional offices proved to be important catalysts for Apicella's multidisciplinary instincts.

Back in London in the early 1980s, the Houston tower project won Apicella a key role working for Piers Gough of CZWG on an alternative to Mies van der Rohe's controversial proposal for Mansion

Top left: Touring Exhibition and Conference Hall for Imagination, 1989. **Left:** *ICL Computers Environment for Spectrum Communications, 1992.* **Opposite:** *Adshel Research & Development Centre, London, 1998.*

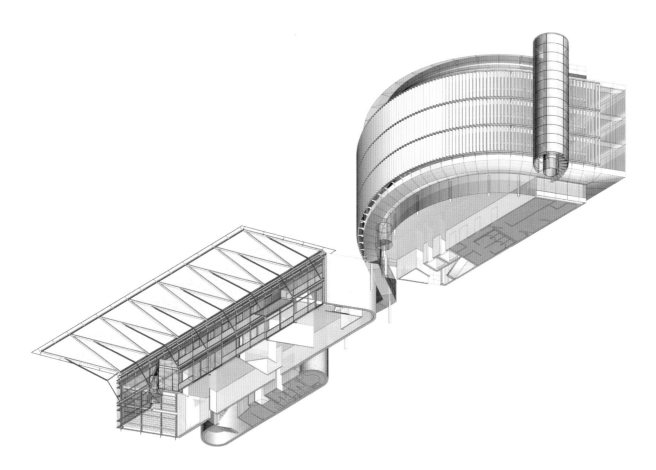

House Square in London. Unashamedly conceived as "an ode to Mies," the scheme was designed as a provocation—a response to the debate between traditional modernists who favored the original Mies scheme and conservationists who wanted to preserve the Victorian character of the site. Apicella's plans, sketches, and perspectives were prominently published in the *Architects' Journal* and exhibited in the Royal Academy Summer Show at precisely the moment when civil war was breaking out in the British architectural community between the modernists and the postmodernists. (In 1984, Prince Charles famously condemned the entire modernist project as a "monstrous carbuncle.")

The Mansion House Square project placed Apicella squarely in the alternative modernist camp. However, although he acknowledges today how influential the heroic phase of modern architecture has been to his work, his relationship with the history of architecture has always been much more complex

than might at first be apparent. Just as he has never disguised his admiration for what he calls the "cerebral depth and precision" of modernism, so Apicella has never hidden either a keen interest in the historical grain of cities, or a more flamboyant side that has enabled him to experiment with folly and spectacle, with sensuality at scale. Looking at his body of work, it becomes apparent that Apicella is motivated by the real history of architecture in all its manifestations, not by a stylistic pastiche of architectural history.

While many of his contemporaries were painting the town in pink granite, putting Greco-Roman jukeboxes on the skyline, Apicella was finding in a stubborn adherence to modernism a route toward

Above: Computer rendering of the Adshel Research & Development Centre (left) and Clear Channel International building (right). **Opposite:** *Various views and details of the Clear Channel International building, London, 2003.*

an architecture that could be more authentic and contemporary. He discovered that modernism's planar vocabulary could be reconfigured as a platform for action, as the space of theater. That allowed him to add an experiential dimension to the geometries of his Miesian mentors.

The three years Apicella spent working as a design associate with Imagination, a live-events and exhibitions company in the mid-1980s, added a further twist. Imagination's in-house guru was Ron Herron, who had pioneered portable architecture in the 1960s with his "Walking City" work for Archigram, and its main client was Ford. There Apicella embarked on a series of spectacular projects, creating portable, lightweight structures that could fold out of trailers and create sophisticated Ford environments in different American cities.

This was live-event architecture on a grand scale, layering a confident design showmanship onto a rational engineering approach, and this specialism would continue as a mainstay of Apicella's own practice, which was set up in 1989 and flourished during the 1990s. Apicella even designed the launch event for Pepsi Blue in an aircraft hangar at Gatwick Airport, an occasion graced by Cindy Crawford riding onstage on a Harley Davidson. Jean-Jacques Lequeu would surely have approved.

Out of the tradition of architectural follies and the street theater of agitprop, a new version of the archetype was emerging—one ideally suited to contemporary conditions and Apicella's talents. An influential article entitled "Welcome to the Experience Economy" in the *Harvard Business Review* (July–August 1998) alerted businesses worldwide to an emerging paradigm.

In their Harvard paper, authors B. Joseph Pine II and James H. Gilmore observed: "Economists have typically lumped experiences in with services but experiences are a distinct economic offering, as different from services as services are from goods." They also pointed out that whereas goods are made

and services are delivered, experiences are staged. Similarly, goods are tangible, services intangible, but experiences are memorable; goods are standardized, services customized, but experiences personal; goods are inventoried, services delivered on demand, but experiences revealed over a duration; and goods have features, services have benefits, but experiences have sensations.

Viewed within the context of the "experience economy," Apicella's work immediately takes on a special meaning. What Apicella revels in is a rare ability at place making in order to create memorable experiences, staged over a duration and offering personal sensations. Some might even interpet this place making as a quest to reconnect with the most perfect place of all: his Italian birthplace, Ravello.

Apicella can take a place that seemingly defies logic and make it a sane oasis in the city for its users, as in his brilliantly shielded campus for street advertising firm Clear Channel/Adshel on one of London's busiest arterial roads. He can animate an unpromising place by use of form, color and light so that people discover it, as they do in Investigate, the permanent exhibition space he designed as part of the Clore Centre for Education in the basement of the Natural History Museum. Or he can create a memorable place entirely independent of site, as in his spectacular touring pavilion for the Hong Kong Tourist Authority.

These three projects illuminate different aspects of Apicella's art. The Clear Channel/Adshel project, for example, required the contradictory impulses of framing and shelter to address a noisy, polluted, and problematic site sandwiched between Philbeach Gardens and the West Cromwell Road in Earls Court, London. The position is one of Europe's most lucrative street-advertising sites, but behind the road-facing billboards, Apicella was required to build a prestigious research-and-development center capable of entertaining city mayors and demonstrating street furniture in a calm, protected environment.

To achieve all this, Apicella's sense of composition was masterful. Phase 1 of the project—a 7,000-square-foot, light, glazed pavilion building sitting in a secluded garden with its back to the main road—was completed by Apicella Associates in 1999. Phase 2, completed in 2003 by Pentagram, extends

*Far left (top and bottom): Investigate interactive science facility for children, Clore Centre for Education, Natural History Museum, London, 2000. **Left** (top and bottom): Assembly area, Clore Centre for Education, Natural History Museum, London, 2000.*

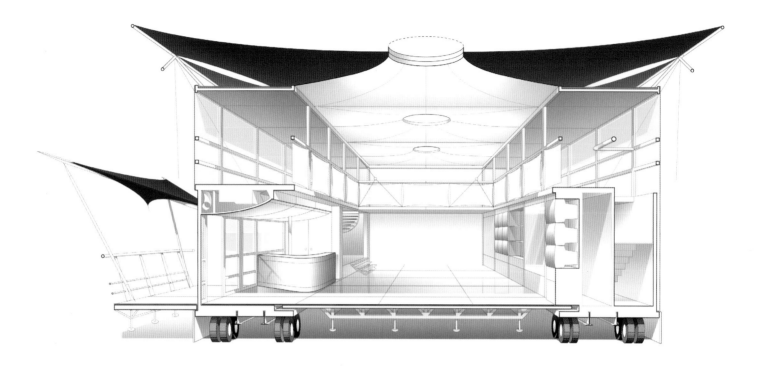

the campus with a five-story curved building at the edge of the site, offering 17,000 square feet of additional studio and office accommodation, and a series of five apartments, each 500 square feet.

The ensemble is completed by an illuminated service tower facing onto a small public garden at the edge of the site and acting as a public landmark for the millions of cars streaming in and out of central London. What ties the entire campus together is the rational, modernist, "white-tech" language of its architecture and the way it conducts a dialogue with its context, the massing of the new curved building not only reflecting the scale of terraced housing alongside but also relating to Michael Aukett's handsome Tesco store opposite.

The Clore Centre for Education at the Natural History Museum, completed by Pentagram in 2000, offered a different set of site-specific problems. A narrow 5,000-square-foot basement space struggling for natural light was poorly oriented in relation to the museum. Would visitors even know it was there?

Apicella's approach was to view the space in relation to the museum's core circulation routes, to connect it to the master plan. Thus the facility was confidently advertised with a futuristic silver-paneled portal at the ground-floor level to encourage visitors to venture down to the basement.

Downstairs the project reveals itself in two parts. The Investigate gallery, a hands-on center for a classroom of thirty-two children to interact with natural objects as well as surf the Web at four large tables, adjoins an assembly area with supporting seminar spaces. Apicella decided to animate the entire center with a ripple effect of color and light against a backdrop of honey-colored bricks, the result of stripping back the interior to Alfred Waterhouse's original building shell. The scheme exemplifies Apicella's place within Pentagram as an architect, his crisply delineated interior design

Above and opposite: Computer rendering and view of traveling-exhibition pavilion for the Hong Kong Tourist Authority, 1997.

complementing partner Angus Hyland's graphics to turn a study in gloom into an animated destination.

The foldaway Hong Kong tourist pavilion, completed by Apicella Associates in 1995, had no intractable site issues to generate a design response. The brief was to promote Hong Kong as a travel destination to holidaymakers and conference organizers in fifty European cities in a year—and the client's original idea was to bring over a Hong Kong tram and park it outside hired venues.

Apicella's background in portable architecture, refined on projects for Ford and TSB Bank, gave the Hong Kong Tourist Authority an alternative strategy. He created a modern steel-and-glass pavilion capable of "growing" with the use of hydraulics from two standard forty-foot truck trailers into a structure four times their original volume. The use of a fabric membrane in combination with a lightweight aluminium structure was deliberate, explained Apicella, to reflect the traditional and modern character of Hong Kong in an abstract way—its high-tech industry as well as an evocation of the junk sails in Hong Kong Harbor.

The pavilion, which appeared to turn by stealth from a chrysalis into a butterfly, was also designed to withstand extremes of temperature—Spain at the height of summer, Switzerland in the depths of winter. Apicella first set up his Hong Kong pavilion in Battersea Park before sending the show on the road. Wherever it went, this piece of environmental product design carried a powerful communication campaign, while also creating an architectural sense of space.

In creating a memorable experience for everyone who visits, the Hong Kong pavilion is the kind of project that crystallizes Apicella's appeal. And in its mix of hybrid creativity, artistic messaging, and technical precision, it also appeals directly to Apicella's Italian roots, making the question "Would you call yourself a designer or an architect?" recede from view—like one of Apicella's ingenious pavilions folding out of sight.

Design Diplomacy

Kurt Weidemann on *Justus Oehler*

"All form admits of a certain beauty, because no form can be so clearly determined by its purpose that does not leave a little to the imagination."

Friedrich Schiller

DISREGARDING THE FACT that man has engaged in decorative, creative activity for millennia, the brief history of the design professions does not span much more than a century. Within that period, these professions, which were originally of a primarily artistic nature, have undergone quite a considerable transformation.

At the turn of the last century, Henri de Toulouse-Lautrec was still pursuing both his vocation as an artist and his profession as an applied graphic designer. A drawing without script was considered to be art; a drawing with script on a poster was graphic design—though it wouldn't formally be identified as such for another half century. Knowledge of the past, its transformations and intellectual heritage, also stands us in good stead for the future. We get a better view if we stand on our fathers' shoulders than if we stand on our own two feet.

We have to learn to look, just as we have to learn to find ideas and to give things form and color. Overall, the distinction between specialist and generalist design has led to the development of increasingly knowledge-based professions. More and more, brand designers, illustrators, photographers, product designers, trade fair and exhibition designers, IT specialists, and new-media designers are collaborating on complex projects. Consortia of varying composition cooperate across boundaries and continents on individual and joint projects.

Pentagram Design Limited, established in London, is one such consortium, an association of practicing designers—who, while operating within a contemporary culture of interdisciplinary cross-fertilization, still pride themselves on their craftsmanship. The partnership embraces all aspects of design, maintaining exacting, ambitious standards, and has enjoyed continuous, controlled growth.

In the London of the 1960s, anyone who wanted to see good design had to go to Fletcher, Forbes & Gill—the founders of the Pentagram concept—where the standards for quality and responsibility were set, and still apply. Today, "good" design doesn't only refer to canonical products, as it did in those early days when the profession was establishing, explaining, and justifying its existence. Today, good design is

Opposite: New look for Faber & Faber's poetry series, 2001.

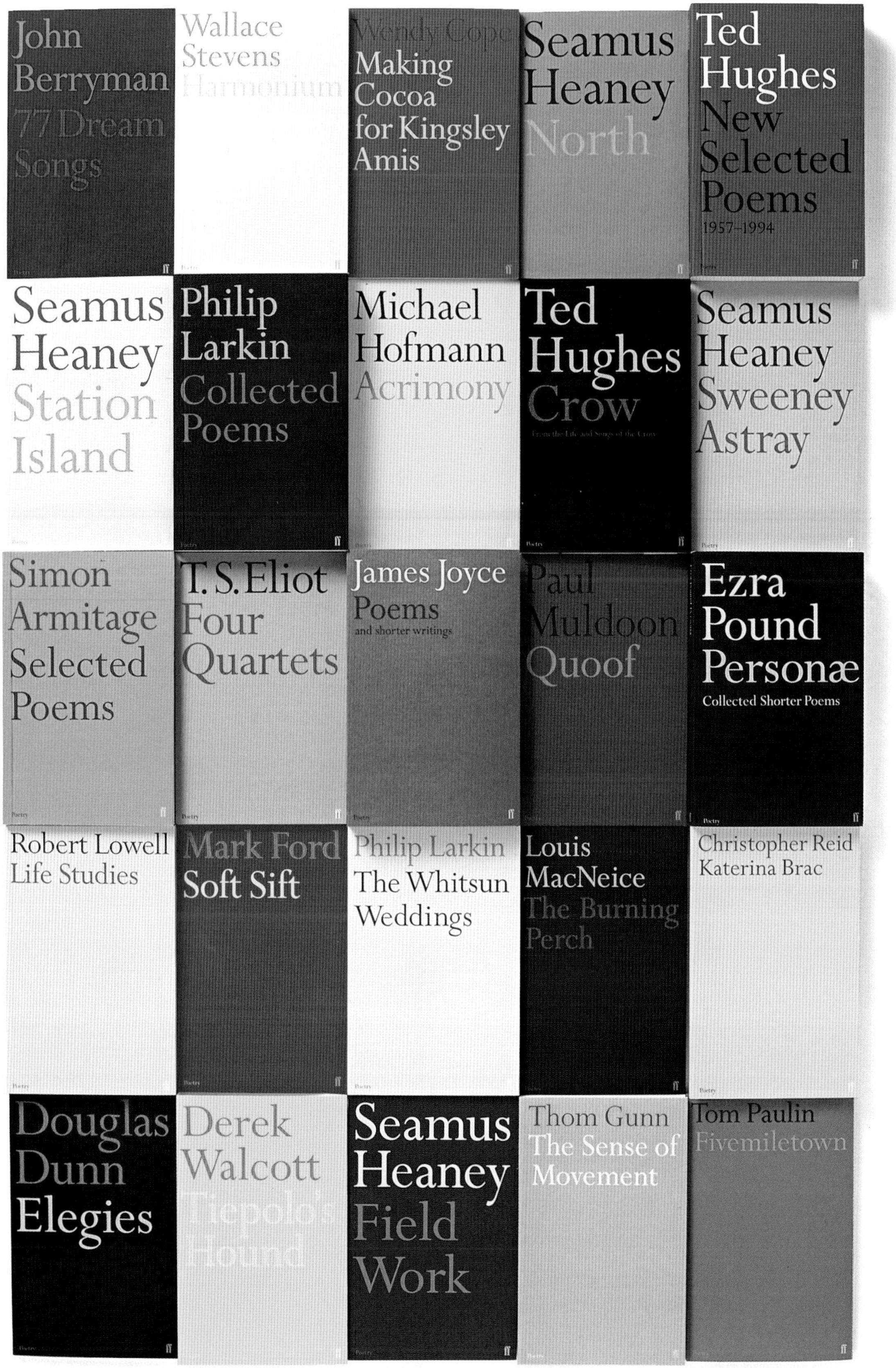

John Berryman 77 Dream Songs	Wallace Stevens Harmonium	Wendy Cope Making Cocoa for Kingsley Amis	Seamus Heaney North	Ted Hughes New Selected Poems 1957–1994
Seamus Heaney Station Island	Philip Larkin Collected Poems	Michael Hofmann Acrimony	Ted Hughes Crow From the Life and Songs of the Crow	Seamus Heaney Sweeney Astray
Simon Armitage Selected Poems	T. S. Eliot Four Quartets	James Joyce Poems and shorter writings	Paul Muldoon Quoof	Ezra Pound Personæ Collected Shorter Poems
Robert Lowell Life Studies	Mark Ford Soft Sift	Philip Larkin The Whitsun Weddings	Louis MacNeice The Burning Perch	Christopher Reid Katerina Brac
Douglas Dunn Elegies	Derek Walcott Tiepolo's Hound	Seamus Heaney Field Work	Thom Gunn The Sense of Movement	Tom Paulin Fivemiletown

STAR ALLIANCE

also about interdisciplinary, international networks. Good designers cooperate with one another and collaborate with their clients to offer consistent quality.

Justus Oehler, one of the nineteen Pentagram partners, embodies this attitude within design. He produces his projects in close collaboration with his clients' decision makers. He is capable of what Bertolt Brecht expected of a good playwright: "thinking with other people's heads." The complexities of the corporate design project for the international airline network Star Alliance, involving fifteen airlines from a wide variety of cultures and bringing to the table a wide variety of corporate cultures, can be mastered only by a designer who also acts as a consultant designer. The symbol is a dynamic star made of individual elements that reflect the diversity of the alliance. It is simple, understandable, recognizable, and timeless. And thanks to a diplomatic design solution, it does not compete in any way with the other existing airline logos and identities: The dominant color of the Star Alliance identity is black, a color that is not used by any of its member airlines. It was this aspect of his design solution which was the one most difficult to sell to the client at first because of the negative connotations black has in most cultures, but which in the end helped make Star Alliance extremely visible. Since its launch six years ago Oehler has been acting as design and brand consultant to the Star Alliance.

Process—what some see as that intermediary stage before closure—is for Oehler the core activity of design. By making process, in essence, the product, he insures not just ongoing control over his work but a more meaningful relationship with his clients. Case in point: He has been with Star Alliance longer than any of its constituent members. He is the holder of knowledge. And, not incidentally, passion. Recently, when the Polish airline LOT joined the consortium, Oehler was flown to Warsaw to brief the newest member of the Alliance on the Star identity: its implementation, its psychology. Oehler the designer was cast as Oehler the emissary; the client felt only he had the persuasive "passion" to ensure the brand would be properly perpetuated.

Left: Star Alliance logo, 1996. **Opposite:** *New promotional livery for Star Alliance, 2003.*

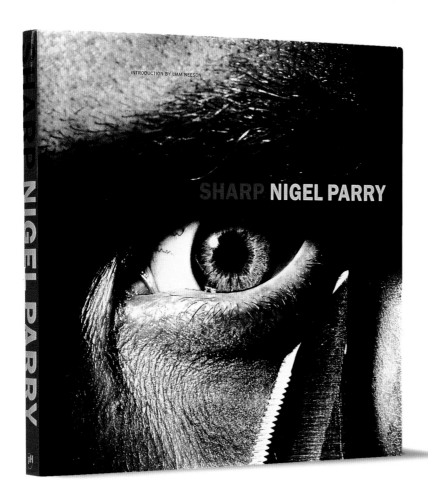

Consultant designers like Oehler acquire an authority and influence that help to define business processes beyond mere marketing measures. Complementing (some might say surpassing) the reflective thought processes of decision makers accustomed to working exclusively with figures, he is able to give immediate form to the intuitive: In other words, his work is striking, comprehensible, and self-sufficient.

Oehler, who as a middle child experienced politics and diplomacy from a very early age, today enjoys the challenges of complex multicultural and politically sensitive projects such as the afore-mentioned Star Alliance, the World Economic Forum, Citibank, and the International Labour Organization (ILO). He enjoys the challenge of the creative phase as much as that of implementation and ongoing consultancy. But he also loves short-term, high-speed projects requiring spontaneous solutions. In his book-jacket designs for Faber & Faber he demonstrates the intelligence of his interpretative skills. *Sharp*, the Nigel Parry book for powerHouse Books, reveals Oehler's mastery of the devices of design, allowing him to handle the impressive portrait photographs on consistently equal terms with the text. A highly challenging image was created for the Museum für Post und Kommunikation in Germany: simple and colorful, inviting, and avoiding the values of monumentality and grandiosity historically associated with the institution of the museum.

Above and opposite: Book design for Sharp: Nigel Parry, *published by powerHouse Books, 2000.*

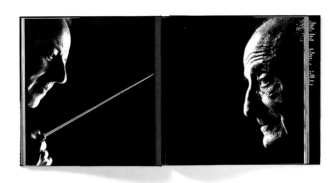

HELP

THEY'RE ALWAYS TRYING TO CENSOR ME... LET'S DO IT LIKE THIS

Justus Oehler experienced life on an international basis before being able to join the Pentagram partnership. He was born in Tokyo, grew up in France and Greece, and studied design in Munich and London. (His father's work for the Goethe-Institut accounts for Oehler's itinerant, cosmopolitan upbringing.) His recent move to Berlin to set up the newest Pentagram office is the closest thing to a homecoming he knows, for Oehler is truly a global citizen. He sees Berlin as a new frontier: a city half-finished, with people flooding to it, highly international with close proximity to the burgeoning Eastern European markets. In short, a place to exponentially increase the scope and boundaries of Pentagram's practice.

There are no difficulties involved in putting together an international, multilingual consortium when its members are in agreement on values, ideas, meaning, and awareness. Design is not distinguished by national or folkloric characteristics—by British fairness, French esprit, or German thoroughness. Design is determined by the nature of the assignment and the needs of the audience. And as political events continually bear out, working cross-culturally is the central task of the twenty-first century. Oehler's work for the International Labour Organization is an ideal case study.

The ILO is the United Nations agency that promotes social justice and internationally recognized human and labor rights. Founded in 1919, it is the only surviving major creation of the Treaty of Versailles, which brought the League of Nations into being. It became the first specialized agency of the UN in 1946. As one might expect, it is also multilingual. Accordingly, its current identity—the ILO logo—is regularly altered by each member nation in order to be legible to their particular constituency. Oehler saw that a different approach to translation was needed, not only to unify the ILO's graphic identity but also to revive an internal sense of common purpose that had become fractured and confused by the proliferation of informal adaptations. Oehler understands design as a political animal that must be able to move fluently across

*Opposite: New look for Faber & Faber's Paul Auster series, 2000. **Right:** New identity for telecom company Tiscali, 2003.*

borders. So his proposal sidesteps the linguistic problem and offers a common symbol that can be paired with the translation of ILO into any language.

Oehler's recognition that borders are elastic but nonetheless real, that cultures are not myths but methods of behavior, has been the key to a more recent project for the Internet service provider Tiscali. A small Sardinian telecom company, Tiscali set out to compete with Telecom Italia. (Apocryphally, Tiscali is the name of the cave where the ancient Sardinians hid from the conquering Romans: Its opening became synonymous with freedom.)

The first to offer free Internet access in Italy, Tiscali saw its share value skyrocket. Through a rapid succession of mergers and acquisitions, it has become a pan-European company, with operations in fourteen different countries. It bought seven ISPs in Germany alone. The resulting combination of languages—corporate and cultural—is staggering, and it's taking its toll on the corporate brand: Different localities have started retooling what was to begin with a very relaxed corporate identity. Oehler's challenge has been to convince Tiscali of the need to involve those localities in the formation of the new identity—if only by visiting them himself. He knows that the successful implementation of whatever he designs depends on the extent to which Tiscali's members feel like they belong to the same group. He also knows that the culture of Tiscali's founders is in spirit, and by nature, still Sardinian, still attached to the iconography of the cave. By attending to each of these cultures, not sentimentalizing them, Oehler will complete the task of incorporation, graphically.

Of course, Pentagram designers are not primarily sales promoters—within or outside the client company, as the case may be. That is better left to the marketing experts. But where quality is a prerequisite for success, design is a prerequisite for quality. Content must be translated in its essence, not merely reproduced. If a design is simplified, objectified, and made human, it must be explained rationally—and implemented emotionally. Oehler's work for Tiscali illustrates the criticality of those so-called soft aspects that are essential to solid design.

Pentagram partners are expected to contribute managerial and coaching skills. Ambitious designs frequently go further than the wishes and ideas of clients such as the International Labour Organization and Tiscali. Designers must be able to argue convincingly and to communicate new opinions and attitudes, as with Star Alliance. Purely economic advantages and rational thinking alone are no match for the attitude behind high-quality, artistically inspired design, as with Faber & Faber. Creativity, not of the roving kind, but always at the ready, is what lies behind Pentagram's prestigious reputation. Ideas are planned, organized, made communicable, and realized in a stimulating way. That is Pentagram's culture mirrored in Justus Oehler's culture of design.

Opposite: New identity for the Museum für Post und Kommunikation, Germany, 1995.

Rainmaker

Mike Hicks on *Lowell Williams*

ONE OF MY FAVORITE CHARACTERS, legendary Houston oilman Glenn McCarthy, was known to be able to charm the pants off a snake, especially when soliciting investors. Though Lowell Williams may never evolve into a full-blown Jett Rink clone, there's nonetheless an unmistakable bit of the Texas oilman lurking somewhere within him. It's most visible in the grand gestures that occasionally surface during the course of business and in his "live large" Texas persona.

While he prefers winning business through competence alone, if push comes to shove, Lowell is perfectly capable of landing a deal by leveraging his considerable wit and charm. To contend with Coca-Cola's anxiety about Pentagram's distance from Atlanta, for instance, he sent life-size cardboard cutouts of himself and New York partner Michael Bierut holding a carton of Coke: a whimsical yet serious gesture to underscore their commitment to be readily available whenever needed. It's the type of clever, eleventh-hour gamesmanship Lowell's known for.

Still, peers and clients alike will inevitably refer first to his reasoning, thoroughness, and design skills, revealing considerable substance beneath the down-home Texas style. For as formidable a businessman as he is, he is an equally adept designer.

Lowell develops concepts in a cryptic pictographic language of his own creation, usually devising shorthand diagrams on the spot that chart relationships among ideas, processes, and products. These describe in hierarchical order the entire process, from problem descriptions to the formulation of solutions and the means of attaining them. It's second nature to him and integral to his personal design process. Although he finds his scribblings perfectly decipherable, the untrained eye could easily mistake them for genealogical charts drawn by monkeys on amphetamines. Hence, note taking during his accompanying explanation is strongly recommended to anyone lacking a photographic memory.

That said, the key to understanding Lowell as a designer is to understand that these diagrams, first and foremost, provide a necessary context for his creative efforts.

Opposite: Detail from the Gutenberg Bible display at the Harry Ransom Center, University of Texas at Austin, 2003.

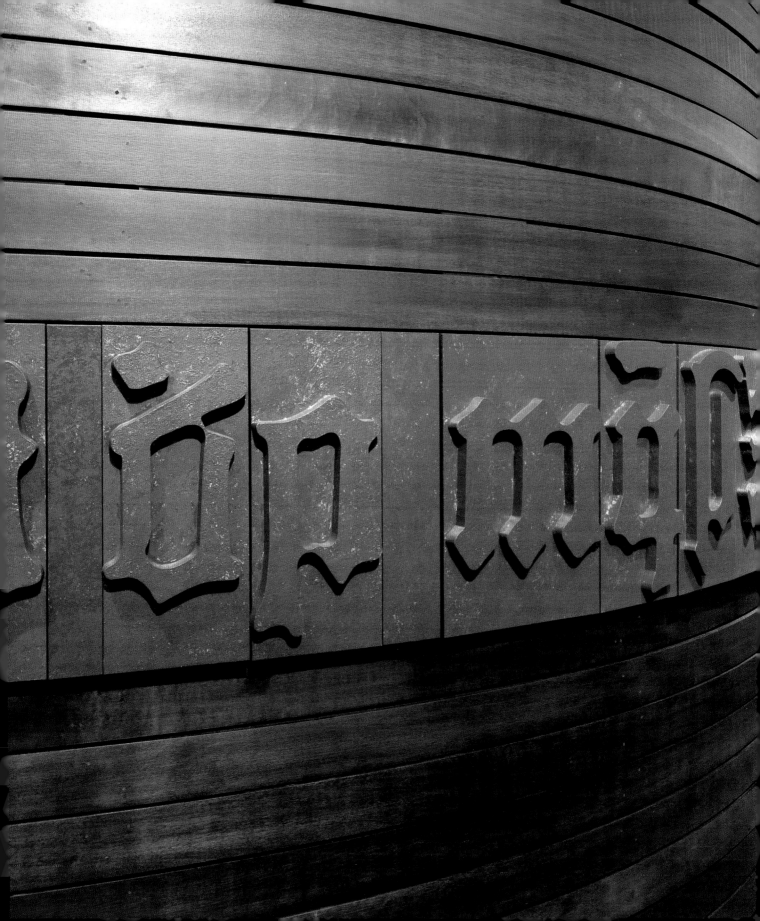

Lowell is goal oriented. You know, check off the list; reassign new tasks; move the ball forward. That's his way. I don't believe he can process information without first arranging and prioritizing it into some sequential order. All of which endears him greatly to business types with unwieldy or complicated projects. If it's so complex and oblique that only a team of idiots savants can explain it, then Lowell is your guy.

One of his huge strengths as a designer is that he can take a vast amount of information and present it in a very clear, logical, and elegant manner. "I didn't start out to be that kind of designer. It just evolved," says Lowell. "However, I know exactly where the evolution started—when I went to work with Saul Bass in Los Angeles."

Though known widely for his film titles and identity programs, within his profession Saul Bass was regarded as the undisputed master of design presentations and the corporate sell. Lowell's approach to getting a job with Saul was typically direct: He simply answered an ad in the back of *Communication Arts* magazine for a senior art director. When Saul subsequently offered to fly him out for an interview, it was the first time he had been on an airplane outside Texas. Being Lowell, he reviewed all airlines and flights from Houston to LA, then selected the one with the most stops so he could experience taking off and landing as many times as possible between the two cities. With the help of then-fledgling Continental Airlines, he was able to manage five takeoffs and five landings both going and coming. By his reasoning, this was a splendid way to see the country and become a veteran flyer in merely one journey. Even by Lowell's standards, it was a very long, though productive, day.

It's still indicative of the way Lowell approaches assignments, using opportunities to realize multiple goals, though now he generally does it on behalf of clients and flies direct.

Lowell credits his marketing savvy to working for Saul. "I had the opportunity to work on very complex, high-stakes identity programs for the likes of AT&T and Warner Communications. Most all of the projects that came through Saul's office required you to use both sides of your brain. Using just the creative side was never an option."

Above: Exhibition space for permanent display of the Gutenberg Bible at the Harry Ransom Center, University of Texas at Austin, 2003. Opposite: Exhibition design for In the Light, *the inaugural exhibition at the renovated Harry Ransom Center, 2003.*

124

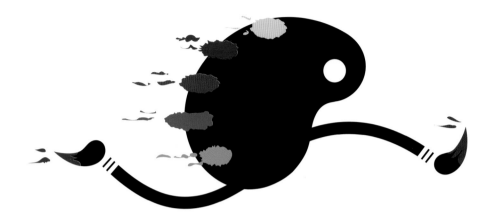

In the late 1970s, Lowell returned to Houston to open his own studio. "The timing could not have been better. Houston was on the cusp of two economic booms: oil and real estate," says Lowell. "Our big break came through our work with real-estate developer Gerald Hines. Hines was one of the first to hire top-name architects—Philip Johnson, I. M. Pei, Kevin Roche, Robert A. M. Stern, Cesar Pelli—to design large-scale, largely speculative commercial projects. We quickly found ourselves working beside very high-profile architects on very high-profile projects in virtually every major city in the US. Major-league stuff.

"Great importance and big bucks were put on the marketing programs because we basically were selling high-priced office space in buildings that didn't exist. To put things in perspective, more than once we custom-made paper for brochures that mimicked a building's stone; we developed photographic techniques to show buildings in their real settings years before they were built—and we did it without the benefit of today's digital processes.

"We made a market, I guess," Lowell says, adding, "It was a really great time to be in the design business." Working with legendary architects wasn't all that bad either. "While I've always liked architecture," Lowell says, he never wanted to be an architect. "It is always much more fun to come in, get involved in the design process without having to worry that something is going to fall down. One of the lessons I took away from this experience is the value of collaboration among design disciplines—architecture, engineering, graphic design," he says. "A few years later, the idea of collaborating with other designers became a motivating factor for joining Pentagram."

When Lowell joined Pentagram San Francisco in 1991, he found a venue totally suited to his skills, the proverbial key to the candy store.

"The Pentagram name is a business magnet," he points out, smiling and rubbing his hands together like a kid on Christmas morning. He stayed in San Francisco for three years before returning to Texas and bringing Pentagram with him.

Pentagram grows when a partner moves. "We don't have a master plan, but if we had one, Austin

*Above: Identity for Race for the Arts fundraising event, Austin Museum of Art, 2000. **Opposite:** Identity for Taco Bueno restaurants, Texas, 1998.*

wouldn't be on it. Still, here we are. I like to joke that Austin is Pentagram's outlet-mall location," he quips. "For whatever reasons, some people think that maybe we're the more accessible or the least intimidating office. And, of course, we are. We're in Texas, in Austin, where everyone is laid back, where there is music and barbecue and recreation. It's the polar opposite of any of our other offices. I could have gone anywhere, but this is where I want to live. And while we don't get a lot of work in Austin, we split the coasts, making everywhere an easy commute." So being a "Ferrari in a pickup town," Lowell's first take on setting up shop in Austin, works just fine.

(You will find that automotive analogies pepper Lowell's conversations. He is, indeed, a certified car and motorcycle fanatic. One of his first questions to job candidates is what color car they own. A correct answer here can go a long way toward a job offer. Hint: Lowell believes cars should be either black or white, though he recently added red as a concession to Pentagram. Anyone owning beige transport would be well advised to arrive on foot.)

A good portion of what Lowell does these days used to fall under the broad category of account service in the advertising business. Sadly, this level of account service is all but extinct in the ad industry now, mostly because it requires the practitioner to command the respect of the client. Agencies, for the most part, have become far too sycophantic to garner such authority and, in any event, are trusted less than bankers. Hence, this function has moved into the domain of business consultants and active board members, the former usually being myopic number crunchers, the latter loose cannons on management's decks. Lowell and Pentagram represent an attractive third option: independent professionals with deep resources, hands-on experience, and a healthy disregard for generic hyperbole.

The distinction is crucial. In Lowell's view, Pentagram bridges the gap between traditional business consulting and marketing or advertising. Consequently, while a growing portion of what he does could correctly be construed as business consulting, it almost always results in a deliverable product. In actual practice, the process and decisions it creates are evidenced in the final product, and I've always been impressed with how seamlessly the process infuses his design.

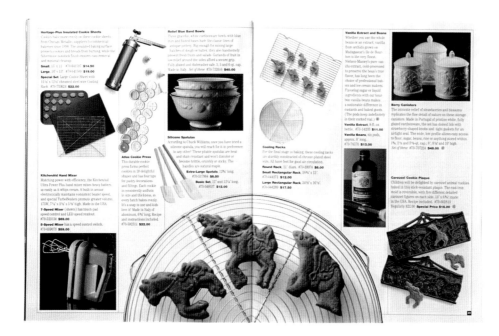

Not surprisingly, over the last five years, this has led to projects far outside the realm of print, from strategic planning and naming for start-ups to direct merchandising, national identity programs, packaging, exhibitions, signage, even architectural concept development.

Of all the projects Pentagram has produced, the Williams-Sonoma catalog for cooks may be the most widely seen and used. Lowell has worked with W-S for more than a decade, and the relationship has only strengthened over the years. "It's the only business that gives you an instant report card," he says. "I love that."

A few years ago, W-S was considering expanding their product offering "beyond the kitchen," a concept that was the subject of much debate. Lowell quickly produced a diagram that featured the kitchen at the center, surrounded by boxes representing all the other rooms in a house that touch the kitchen. His advice: "If it doesn't touch the kitchen, it shouldn't be part of the product mix." As soon as the buyers saw it mapped out on kraft paper, they understood the reasoning and bought into the concept. This insight helped maintain the company's identity and gave a logical focus to successive expan-

sion. Is this the traditional definition of design? No. Is it valuable? You bet.

As a designer, Lowell is the polar opposite of the cliché of the chaotic, emotional artiste. His is design born of reason and order. While there's clearly a muse somewhere within that guides his process, it's so deeply embedded as to be invisible to most outsiders. To them it seems like everything just falls into place on its own with astonishing regularity—which is just fine with Lowell. This is wonderfully comforting to corporations with lots of money riding on the outcome of marketing programs. The method often begins on a very fundamental level.

"What I always look for with any client," says Lowell, is their 'stake in the ground.' What are their assets? What do they absolutely own that they can base successive efforts on?"

In the case of Disney, Lowell wound up defining the stake in the ground at a moment when the company's merchandise catalog lacked a clear visual direction. In his signature distill-to-the-essence approach, Lowell convinced them that their mer-

*Above: Spread from catalog for kitchenware retailer Williams-Sonoma, 1994. **Opposite**: Spread from catalog for Disney, 2001.*

chandise was lost in decoration and contended that Disney's DNA was defined by the character Mickey Mouse, the beloved rodent inextricably tied to all things Disney. Thus Mickey became the focus for the catalog's creative theme.

Like many of Lowell's insights, this one seems much simpler and more obvious in retrospect. But as he points out, "Sometimes it takes an outsider to give credibility to the obvious.

"Disney has such a strong heritage and culture," he says. "Hey, I grew up watching *The Mickey Mouse Club*. This was like working with a star. The best thing we could do was reinstate Mickey to heroic status and keep everything else out of the way." …which is what happened. Over the course of a year, Lowell and his team worked with Disney to re-concept and redesign the catalog until the new direction was firmly in place.

"While I'll always enjoy print," Lowell says, his focus of late has been on architecture-related projects: exhibitions, signing, and architectural concepting. "Many of these projects afford us the opportunity to work with our own partners. Multi-disciplined projects are a perfect match for Pentagram's broad range of resources and expertise.

While a few of my colleagues might disagree, two partners are always smarter than one."

Lowell has collaborated with New York partner and architect Jim Biber on several projects, including two restaurant chains, La Salsa and Taco Bueno, for a large restaurant group. Both projects involved repositioning the brand, identity, and packaging, as well as signing and architecture, all at the same time.

"Breaking down the barriers between architecture and graphic design is the best-case scenario for the client," Lowell believes, "because it guarantees a single design proposition and execution across the board."

Coincidentally, as Lowell was developing the Taco Bueno trademark, New York partner Woody Pirtle was in Austin collaborating on another project. So he asked Woody to do a drawing for a concept using the letterforms in the word "taco" to create a face. Woody took the drawing home, where his wife, Leslie, saw it. A designer herself, she suggested using a speech balloon to contain the word "bueno," thus creating the whimsical, self-endorsing Taco Bueno trademark/mascot the chain's owners have come to love. I believe it may be the first time, other than in a nightclub, that a collaborator

has collaborated with a collaborator's collaborator unknowingly and emerged the better for it.

Exhibition design has also presented collaborative opportunities. Lake/Flato Architects called Pentagram in on the Harry Ransom Center at the University of Texas at Austin. Lowell found the project particularly exciting, "in part," he says, "because of the breadth of the collection [everything from one of the few remaining Gutenberg Bibles to the original script for *Gone with the Wind*, what is thought to be the world's first photograph, plus some thirty-six million manuscripts, five million photographs, a million books, and more than one hundred thousand works of art and design] and in part because you have the opportunity to bring storytelling to life."

As with everything else, Lowell has pared down his business philosophy to a simple but unbreakable rule: A project must involve two of the following three conditions: (1) compelling work, (2) outrageous fees, and (3) an extraordinarily good person to work with as a client.

Opposite: Identity and architecture for La Salsa restaurants, USA, 2003. Above: Commemorative jersey for the Lance Armstrong Foundation Golf Invitational, Austin, Texas, 2002.

"Occasionally we get the perfect project, one with all three," smiles Lowell. "But I am quite content with two. And in fact, that's where most of the business is. Any time a project dips to only one, something's wrong. Then you either repair the relationship or rethink it."

Because Pentagram is an amalgam of successful and forceful personalities, there is always the possibility of the annual partners' meeting devolving into something resembling nineteen wolverines dividing a chicken pizza. Hence, more than a few partners have alluded to the value of Lowell's consensus-building skills.

"The British partners think of him as a cowboy," suggests Austin partner DJ Stout. "But Lowell is a good listener, so good in fact that when he does finally speak, people tend to pay attention. He distills information in real time and says what he really thinks. This may be abrasive to some, but you always know where you stand."

The cowboy analogy is not entirely inapt, but I still think Lowell fits better the classic mold of a Texas oilman: smart and independent, with a down-home edge and a genuine gift for making a deal. Of course, no one loves a Texas oilman more than his partners, and no one hates him more than his competitors. I suspect Lowell can live with that.

131

Designer =
Editor =
Curator =
Collaborator =
Designer

Lorraine Wild on *Abbott Miller*

A SURE INDICATOR THAT THE NEWSSTAND one may be perusing is not merely good but great would be the presence of the oddly titled journal *2wice*. However, finding *2wice* somewhere on that newsstand is an exercise in free association: It might be shelved with the art magazines, the photography journals, the decorating magazines, the design magazines, the performing-arts magazines, the academic journals— I've even found it in the self-help section. *2wice* used to carry the subtitle "visual/culture/document," which is probably what started the whole newsstand confusion; now it helpfully adds "visual and performing arts." Oh.

So what's inside? A recent issue (vol. 6, no. 2, 2002) entitled "Glow" appears to address not merely the subject of light but also that of the condition of glowing. The inside cover carries engravings of old lightbulbs printed in hot yellow on cool gray; this is followed by old postcards of early skyscrapers lit up for night; and then more lightbulbs. An introduction connects the subject of nighttime illumination with the spectacle of performance. There are essays on the development of stage lighting, on urban "spectaculars" such as moving billboards, and Day-Glo pigments. In the middle, a set of images of the Montreal-based dance company O Vertigo showing a dancer against a monumental glowing dress; then, a set of photographic portfolios of fireflies, *Star Wars* figurines (light sabers!), more lightbulbs, barbershop poles, and finally a set of out-of-focus reflections of light in the city, which manage to be simultaneously romantic and severely realistic, beautiful *and* critical of the entire giddy enterprise.

To simply list the contents of any given issue of *2wice* describes only half of what you are seeing (and maybe that's what the cryptic title refers to: that it is not only the content but the content as it should be reconsidered through its re-presentation). The journal is modestly sized, somewhere around 100 to 128 pages, and although early issues used to contain more exotic vellum or textured papers bound into the book, recent issues seem to adhere to standard paper and offset printing. But the editorial direction of each issue of *2wice* wanders far beyond

Opposite: Cover of the "Picnic" issue of 2wice *magazine, 2002.*

VISUAL AND PERFORMING ARTS   VOL 6 · NO 1

the generic specification of "journal" into a territory where there are very few precedents. The ideas presented in each issue of *2wice* cannot be separated from their visual documentation. Centered around dance and spinning out into the larger culture, each issue's editorial performance is an intricate choreography of the temporal and the static; photography and typography both capturing and representing the uniquely wide-ranging theme of each issue.

To navigate any given issue of *2wice* is to engage in the same sense of free-association that one might have had to use to track it down in the first place. Classification is elusive. And the reward is obvious, though again hard to define. It lies somewhere in the web of interconnectedness between poetry and fact, between individual expressions (as close and particular as the gestures of a dancer's hands) and the visual aggregates of our big and complicated culture. Sampling is the process, and Abbott Miller (listed on the masthead as "Editor/Designer") is the DJ: the mix master of the mysterious "twiceness" of *2wice* that stakes out the true territory of graphic design.

"Editor/Designer" is a title more typical of the tiny, self-publishing realm of zines than of anything one might find on the masthead of a more conventional magazine, and the close collaboration between Abbott Miller and editor in chief Patsy Tarr is also more "alternative" than the high production values of *2wice* suggest. The issues are curated through the choice of photography and artwork associated with a theme developed by Miller and Tarr, often as a response to a set of dance photographs. Miller describes the activity of building and designing stories around the theme as being simultaneously conceptual and visual, i.e., indivisible. "I find that I fill in pieces that are missing, and I am just as likely to want to edit something or to suggest alternatives to content as I am to make visual decisions."

It is that indivisibility that makes *2wice* such a graphic-design fetish object. It is a classic example of the unity of the idea and the image that is idealized but so rarely pulled off; and to watch Miller accomplish that unity over and over is a scenario to make other graphic designers extremely envious. There are only a few precedents for Miller's work on *2wice*, and they are grand: Fleur Cowles's *Flair* from the 1950s, or some aspects of *Show*, art-directed by

Henry Wolf in the 1960's. But the most important is *Portfolio*, a journal that produced only four legendary issues (beginning in 1950) under Alexey Brodovich, who worked by day as the art director of *Harper's Bazaar* from 1939 until the late '50s. In *Modern Magazine Design*, William Owen says that Brodovich championed "the virtue of surprise and dramatic contrast, the constant employment of original and lateral thought in the service of communicating content." It was this same process that he was able to bring to the oversize pages of *Portfolio*, which combined all sorts of cultural subjects. Of course, part of what makes *Portfolio* so distinctive is the authorship implicit in the creation of such a subjective visual narrative; *2wice* shows evidence of the same sort of "voice," the result of Miller's particular analysis, sensibility, skill, and eye.

The issue of authorship in graphic design, or the "designer's voice," is one that has been persistent in the graphic design world since the mid-1990s. The model of graphic design authorship that predates this debate is the one that equates certain "star" designers with artists. But as the design world and design education expanded in the 1990s with a greater awareness of the larger cultural context of how design is produced and consumed, a new consciousness of the history and theory of design and the various ways that designers functioned began to be articulated. In his 1996 essay "The Designer as Author" Michael Rock singled out the design practice of Abbott Miller and Ellen Lupton as exemplary of this new territory of graphic-design authorship. In their early exhibitions and catalogs such as *The Bathroom, the Kitchen and the Aesthetics of Waste* or △□○: *The Bauhaus and Design Theory*, Lupton and Miller used the actual form of graphic design and their own writing to explore their subjects.

It is hard to overstate the impact of Miller and Lupton's work in the early '90s. That this intellectually entrepreneurial work was coming from two graphic designers was shocking. They posed a

---

Opposite: 2wice *magazine, each issue exploring a different theme.* **Top row, from left:** *"Feet" (1997); "Interiors" (1997); "Uniform" (1998).* **Center row, from left:** *"Night" (1999); "Rites of Spring" (2000); "Ice" (2000).* **Bottom row, from left:** *"Camera" (2001); "Glow" (2002); "Animal" (2003).*

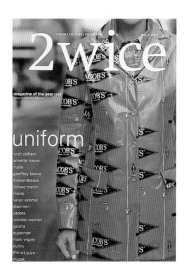

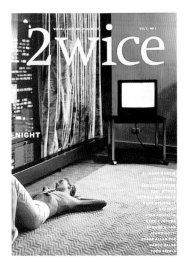

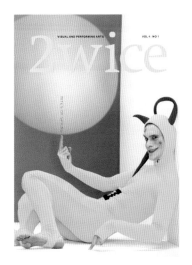

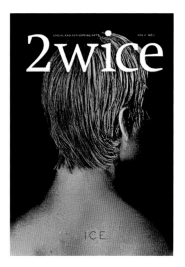

real challenge to prevailing thought, which still tended to focus on the surface of the graphic artifact. Even the name of their collaborative practice, Design/Writing/Research, suggested an intimidating amount of energy and a voracious appetite for work.

"Voice" can be modulated; and Abbott Miller has consistently advocated the use of design to support content. In "The Idea Is the Machine," an essay that he published in *Eye* a decade ago (vol. 10, no. 3, 1993) and which continues to be read by design students, he argues that graphic designers should look at the visual conventions and structures that are under the surface of graphic design as the real site of work, and that the overreliance on the idea of graphic design as a parade of stylistically progressive invention stunts the ability to both see and understand the possibilities for design beyond current practice. Miller's ongoing work as a book designer, particularly his design of exhibition catalogs, provides a clear example of his preference for structure.

Book design is all about conventions: the procession of half titles, titles, copyrights, and contents; the relatively fixed form of the object; and standard printing and binding problems. Art books have an additional layer of conventions driven by notions of the sacrosanct nature of the work of art. It is assumed that their design will be unobtrusive. Miller's work challenges those conventions, not through the surface of the books, but through the book's space and reality as an object.

Miller's design for two very recent exhibition catalogs, *Matthew Barney: The Cremaster Cycle* (Solomon R. Guggenheim Museum, 2002) and *Scanning: The Aberrant Architectures of Diller + Scofidio* (Whitney Museum of American Art, 2003) illustrates this. In both cases, the books document work that has an outrageous visual quality. While the temptation, in another designer's hand, might be to create some visual typographic trope to compete with the work itself, Miller avoids this in favor of exemplifying the ideas in the documented work (and the style of the documentation itself).

Left: Matthew Barney: The Cremaster Cycle, *catalog for the Solomon R. Guggenheim Museum, 2002.* **Opposite:** Scanning: The Aberrant Architectures of Diller + Scofidio, *catalog for the Whitney Museum of American Art, 2003.*

In the Barney book, Miller adapts typographic conventions from encyclopedias, glossaries, and other bibliographic sources to contain the exaggerated amount of information collected on Barney's *Cremaster* film project. These sections flank a "well" of pages devoted to the films themselves accessed via a set of unconventional sculpted tabs. Though the book is over five hundred pages long, the film sections, with their purely visual, uncaptioned sequences of sketches, notes, production photos, props, stills, and associated artworks and installations, fly by in a cinematic flow. The heft of the metallic-satin and vinyl slip-covered tome captures the spectacle of the Guggenheim exhibition while delivering a level of documentation that can actually be accessed.

The typography of both the Barney book and *Scanning: The Aberrant Architectures of Diller + Scofidio* is stylistically similar to all of Miller's work. Clear, structured, correct, using well-crafted contemporary serif and sans serif fonts (the Scala and Quadraat families in particular) Miller's typography works as a delivery system, devoid of any exaggerated expressionistic gestures. In other words, he has a "style," but it is based on the idea not that typography should be invisible or "objective" but that it plays a secondary role to his conceptual responses to the shape and form of the book. In the Diller + Scofidio book, Miller sets up two distinct spaces—the pages of the book itself (which contain the "normal" contents of an exhibition catalog, the analysis of the work, images, etc.) and a whole second set of pages that contain a less rational, more subjectively associated sequence of drawings and photographs. But these pages are hidden. The book is bound with the outer edges of the pages perforated rather than cut, and to access the second space of the book, the reader has to split each page apart. This act of vandalism feels very weird (and is probably responsible for many people's buying two copies), but it exemplifies the both analytical and literal deconstruction embodied in Diller + Scofidio's work.

Right: Harley-Davidson's 100th anniversary Open Road Tour *at the Atlanta Motor Speedway, the first of its ten stops around the world from July 2002 to August 2003.*

Of course, the only way that a designer can participate to this degree of depth is to rearrange the terms' engagement, to be part of the conversation right from the beginning. Miller describes his role as a designer as having a range of possibilities:

"At the lightest (or most subtle) end of the spectrum, I am kind of a 'host' (to images, texts, objects): in the middle zone, I am a kind of 'filter,' influencing the representation and communication by subjecting it to a kind of selective portrayal. At the most authoritarian end, I am a director, with the intimations of either 'auteur' or 'diva' or 'artiste.' In some ways I resist this authoritarian side because it's a cliché, but also because it's an inversion of the 'host' model, it's more like you become a 'host' in the parasitic sense, looking for projects to deploy yourself across, instead of making them true to what they should be."

And this is where Miller's critical intelligence and suppleness (as well as modesty and humor) work in his favor. Who wouldn't trust this guy, a designer genuinely interested in the content he is being compensated to work with, and who is willing to bother to understand it well enough to calibrate the degree of his own intervention? And yet, at the same time, Miller describes himself as always looking for "allowable" moments (such as the thumb tabs on the Matthew Barney book) where he can assert his vision, invent a form: And, of course, he achieves the freedom to do this by aligning his interests (and his solutions) with the concepts of his projects. Miller's version of graphic authorship is far removed from artiste-hood, flexible and collaborative.

The collaborations have moved from the scale of publications to the bigger venue of exhibitions, returning Miller to an aspect of design practice that he had previously engaged in as author/curator/designer, in collaboration with Lupton in Design/Writing/Research. The exhibition is an extension of Abbott Miller's book design at the architectural scale and points to the direction of his future work. Miller says that his current obsession is with "objects, spaces, and interiors... I am constantly amazed by the realities of space and physical conditions. I love books, but there is something more exhilarating about the edgeless conditions of real space."

But maybe an exhibition is the best manifestation of that combination of information, entertainment, and real space. The Harley-Davidson *Open Road Tour* exhibition (July 2002–August 2003) comprised a set of tents festooned with huge words: "myth," "culture," and "machine," not what you'd expect approaching a celebration of such a huge pop-culture icon. But the exhibition was identifiably Miller's, with its celebration of the motorcycle as object in *all* of its manifestations, as technology, as design, as symbol, as phenomen. The formal language of the tents came from the spectacle of racing, the hot oranges and reds, black and white, scaffolding, chrome, and black leather. A central tent devoted to the engines themselves featured a huge tower that looks like a cross between Tatlin's tower and a tornado of words and metal shards. The language of the machine was blown up and romanticized, iconicized. Names of bike models, races, and glorifying song lyrics met in interactive areas where the spectator could mount the icons, try on the leather, rub on tattoos.

Abbott Miller cites the work of Charles and Ray Eames as a historical precedent, their combination of analytical research, organic and optimistic form, and focus on design as a humanistic discipline. While he admits that it is "traditional to honor them," a lot of other designers do the same without actually putting their model to the test. It's 2003, not 1953. The conditions that enabled the Eames no longer exist, but the nature of their "voice" is still a compelling model to look to. Miller's version of graphic-design authorship represents the best of a new attitude in design: engaged with the culture, inflected by theory, enabled by technology, and energized by research.

Opposite: Interior of the Harley-Davidson Open Road Tour's *central "machine" tent.*

The Investigator

Alain de Botton on *John Rushworth*

FOR YEARS, I'D KNOWN AND USED John Rushworth's work without having any clue he was responsible for it or even reflecting (in that ungrateful way most of the public has of approaching design) that any human being had had a hand in it. And yet I'd deeply appreciated the work; its impact had registered in small surges of gratitude and excitement at the presence of unusual beauty in modest things, like noticing a tree blossom in spring or the fragile blue sky on a winter morning. I'd felt pleasure in my local supermarket while stocking up on ready-made meals—Tesco Finest range—and on flicking through my university's post-graduate admissions catalog—King's College, London University. On my honeymoon, I remember admiring the elegance and playfulness of the room-service menu in the Savoy Hotel, and by coincidence, I also remember noting, many years before, the menu in a trendy London Japanese restaurant (Wagamama) while on my first date with the woman who is now my wife (I was too shy to look her in the eye). All along Rushworth had been there in the background, unknown to me, appreciated nevertheless.

When I meet him and tell him this, Rushworth pulls one of his characteristic wry, contented smiles. For him, success as a designer (and he has worked principally in package and graphic design) is all about working quietly behind the scenes and concentrating on letting each object, whatever it may be—a box, a poster, a menu—do its job properly: "I don't like designers who see their work as an excuse to parade their personalities. That's not good design. Good design is about understanding the product and communicating its qualities to the world. Designers shouldn't have an ego." This is vintage John and vintage Pentagram: Buried in this observation is a decided allegiance to the advertising rather than illustrative roots of graphic design.

While it may seem paradoxical to throw a spotlight on a Pentagram partner who believes in the virtues of being forgotten, there is clearly a strong and identifiable philosophy behind all of Rushworth's work, even if that philosophy is one that places responsibility to the personality of the product way above the promotion of any individual

Opposite: Identity for the Bulgari Hotel, Milan, 2004.

stylistic quirks. Perhaps the greatest tribute one could pay to Rushworth is to say that the only common thread binding his disparate portfolio together is a commitment to bringing out the distinctive virtues of whatever object he has been briefed to work on.

When pressed to define his working methods, Rushworth replies: "First and foremost, you have to develop an ability to think and analyze. This is an intellectual job before anything else. Don't believe that intuition will ever deliver magic." This dictum may seem unusual; after all, design is often thought to be more of a visual than an intellectual endeavor: The cult of inspiration is well entrenched in public perception. But Rushworth works in a tradition pioneered by mid-twentieth-century product designers like Henry Dreyfuss who were at pains to take into account the client and consumers' needs—a tradition that sees design as a genuine conversation, not an indulgent monologue. Bringing the same investigative process to graphic design, Rushworth insists that worrying about getting a product to look good should always take second place to a prior and much more important matter: logically and rationally analyzing the particular and not-always-obvious identity of the product. Only through an understanding of its inherent qualities can a good design solution emerge: "If you don't know what's special about the product, then you won't be able to design anything that is appropriate," he tells me. "Of course, it may look pretty, but it won't work—and in this business, if it only looks pretty, it's by definition not working."

Whenever Rushworth is handed a brief, he therefore spends a good deal of time asking questions of a product that could be boiled down to "Who are you?" Of the thousand things one could emphasize in packaging or designing a given product, Rushworth wants to zero in on a few really important ones. What gives this particular ready-meal or brochure or university prospectus or restaurant menu its charm or uniqueness? Rushworth appreciates that our attention span is limited and that

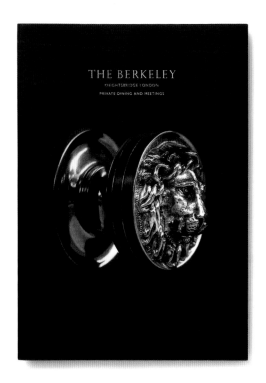

Right: Banqueting brochure for the Berkeley hotel, 1994.
Opposite: Packaging for a set of three CDs designed for the Blue Bar at the Berkeley hotel, London, 2002.

145

successful design demands choices. He is critical of those who overload their designs with meaning, who try to say everything in an overly restricted space and therefore end up confusing rather than enticing audiences. "They're trying to tell you too much because they're nervous," remarks Rushworth. "I take the plunge and aim to tell you the one or two things that actually matter."

One could draw an analogy with the way that a good or bad novelist might set about trying to describe a person. The great novelist picks the three or four salient points that will bring his or her characters to life (think of the character sketches of Austen, Tolstoy, or Proust). The weak novelist will go on for pages describing hair color or family history while still leaving the reader feeling, "Who is this person?" Rushworth has a firm faith that every product, like every person, will have something special that one can say about it, but he's under no illusion that this distinctiveness will be easy to find. And yet a good designer will have to make the eventual design solution seem easy, natural, and inevitable.

A further hurdle in trying to communicate the identity of a product to an audience lies in the way that many companies are themselves rather confused about their ambitions. Therefore, not only are their briefs confused, their entire business models are confused. They don't quite know what they're doing, and their products reflect the drift. Rushworth sees the role of a designer as almost akin to that of a psychoanalyst, a person who can come in and get to know a product better than the product knows itself and thereby help it to come to a sense of its own identity. It isn't surprising to hear that Rushworth spends a lot of time talking to the people who manufacture the products he is asked to design. He'll go to the head office and spend a few days with them, getting to know them informally, chatting to them over lunch, and trying to tease out of them what their particular vision may be. His conversations with his clients often lead him far from the narrow concerns of image-making. He serves as much as a management consultant or business strategist—

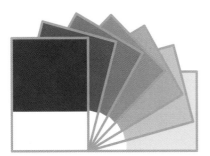

*Left: A new symbol for the color-matching system Pantone, 2000. **Opposite:** Packaging system developed for Pantone with Pentagram partner Daniel Weil, 2000.*

typical of the new professional breed called strategic designers, who, again, grew out of product design, where utility, marketability, and consumer satisfaction are the holy trinity of success. In the course of trying to design a single product, he may end up helping companies to understand their overall aims. No wonder that many of his clients—Boots and the Savoy Group in particular—have valued his input into broader questions of company strategy, perhaps not least because he radiates calm and good sense. (He'd be just the man to have with you if your plane went down on an atoll or to call just after your partner walked out on you.) Rushworth seems to particularly relish the more commercial, entrepreneurial side of the job, and he laments the way that designers have so often been cut off from early consultation on products, because of both a suspicion on the part of managers and the mystique surrounding the design process itself.

Though Rushworth's emphasis on understanding products may sound over-intellectualized, he is far from verbose. It's perhaps not a coincidence that he was born and grew up in Yorkshire, a part of England whose residents are famed for their taciturn and straight-talking nature. Rushworth believes that any understanding he reaches about a product should be capable of expression in just one word or pithy sentence (as he puts it, "It always takes longer to write little"). One of Rushworth's largest projects to date has been an identity redesign for the Savoy Group of luxury hotels in London, and the working methods he employed there are those he will use for almost any project. After studying the three hotels (Claridges, the Savoy, and the Berkeley) over a period of weeks, Rushworth tried to boil down his understanding of the identity of the different establishments to just a single word—like a brand consultant, deciphering the personality

AMANDA WAKELEY

of the product, but with a critical difference. Brand consultants can't give a face to that personality. So the Savoy was distilled to "theatricality," Claridges to "aristocracy," and the Berkeley to "discretion."

Only once he had these key words did Rushworth even begin to think visually: The idea came first, then came an appropriate aesthetic equivalent. With the word in place, he then started to assemble his palette of type and color. With the Savoy, Rushworth went with type that was expressive and celebratory, for gloss, and for bright, contrasting colors: gold, silver, and red. For the Berkeley, Rushworth picked on a pale blue, a restrained, modern font, and a matte look. "I didn't want simply to design any old elegant thing for these hotels. I wanted to understand them. Lasting design relies on understanding." What further distinguishes Rushworth from his counterparts in the branding business is that he avoids the pitfalls of pseudoscience. His work rests somewhere between linear analysis and the nonlinear process of associative thinking. In formulating his palette, he is actually translating behavioral patterns into visible patterns. At that point, clinical analysis gives way to visual common sense—Rushworth's antidote to an overtheorized world.

This approach runs right through Rushworth's work. His most recent project has been a proposed redesign of the diet-food range of the English high-street chemist Boots. When he was initially given the brief, Rushworth sensed some confusion within Boots itself about what they were trying to do with their particular diet range. "There are so many dietary products on the market, I wanted to know what could make the Boots one stand out." To find out, characteristically, Rushworth spent time talking to the people at Boots and sensed that the company saw itself as more medical and scientific than commercial in orientation. While this could be a liability if handled wrongly (it might seem dowdy and depressing), Rushworth also saw a chance to make use of the glamorous and positive associations around science and medicine. He felt that what was special about the Boots diet range was the particular

Left: Identity for fashion brand Amanda Wakeley, 2000.
Opposite: Sculptural monogram for One&Only Resorts, 2002-present.

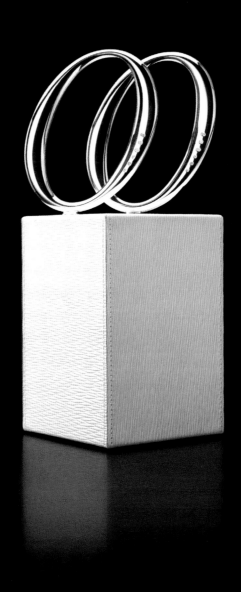

One&Only
Ocean Club
Bahamas

One&Only
Kanuhura
Maldives

One&Only
Le Touessrok
Mauritius

One&Only
Palmilla
Los Cabos, Mexico

One&Only
Royal Mirage
Dubai

The Palace
Arabian Court
Residence & Spa

One&Only
Saratoga
Havana, Cuba

commitment and intelligence of the food scientists who had designed it. "One day I suddenly thought, 'I know what they're making: It's space food for astronauts.'" And so was born the sentence that guided Rushworth in his design of the entire diet range, an understanding that guided him in his choice of all the elements of his palette (cool, elegant, and futuristic).

A side-effect of spending time with Rushworth is that one starts to notice what is wrong with a lot of design. While I'm having lunch with him, my eye is caught by a bottle of mineral water from a Scottish company. My immediate impression is that the bottle is unattractive, but it's only through Rushworthian eyes that I start to understand why this might be. It's because the designer has wanted to convey "Scottishness" without any real grasp of what might be the essential features of the concept. Therefore, the bottle is overloaded with a confusing array of messages: There's a bit of tartan on the label, but also a picture of some heather, an old-fashioned font, and some purple and green motifs. When I ask Rushworth how he would have approached the design task, his answer is what I've come to expect: "I would have gone up to Scotland and met the people bottling this water. I would have tried to see what aspects of Scottish identity really fit the design and which are redundant. I would have left anyone drinking this water with a much surer grasp of what's special about it."

Though Rushworth is, on the surface, admirably modest about what good design can achieve, his vision of his craft is nevertheless at heart very profound. He believes that good design should do nothing less than help us to remember who we are and identify what we want.

Right: Advertisement for One&Only Kanuhura in Vogue *magazine, part of an extensive campaign created by M&C Saatchi, 2003.* **Opposite:** *Brochures for six of the One&Only Resorts, 2002-present.*

Mosaic

John Hockenberry on *Woody Pirtle*

IN THE SUBDUED WORLD of Pentagram's deadlines and deliverables, Woody Pirtle is the bemused hipster. His face is like a weather-beaten Texas road sign— his soul, a mosaic of found wisdom fashioned from shards of fabulous good luck and unimaginable tragedy, a Hank Williams ballad of triumph and woe. On a sunny spring day when the noise of Fifth Avenue shakes the windows at Pentagram's Madison Square nerve center, Woody Pirtle is the calm amid a noisy fishbowl of an office where partners work side by side with all the privacy of a New York subway car. His is a playful, joking tranquility, something like Pan as a martial-arts sensei. Pirtle's particular punch line is an understanding and confidence acquired over more than three decades of experience, delivered with the bemused curiosity that asks, "How did I get here?"

Pirtle's work is immediate and unapologetically visceral. His images demand a popular audience. Pirtle's best images invite play. One can take them apart and put them back together again. They tell stories, and stories are perhaps the key to Woody's populist appeal. He thinks of each piece of work as an invitation to the viewer. There is no broad academic sense of craft in his own personal descriptions of what he does. Instead, it's: Did you get it? Did they get it?

Take the poster art for the Ringling School of Design: an old-style phone with a painter's palette for a dialer bordered by cartoonish lines indicating feverish motion. It's a dramatic, happy image that grabs every component of his client's urgency, needing candidates to call, to have fun. The play on the name: ringing/Ringling is a sophisticated halfrhyme that could have come right out of a Wilfred Owen poem.

But in making a career out of playing to the audience, Pirtle has also lived the aesthetic story line of twentieth-century design: Is it fine art or is it industrial art? This is a question that, generally speaking, would not make for long conversation in the halls of pragmatic Pentagram, or many places outside of them, for that matter, now that graphic design is taken for granted as a profession in its own right. But it remains central for Woody. Artist?

Opposite: Poster for Amnesty International, 2001.

STOP GUN TRAFFICKING

NO MORE GUNS FOR TORTURE AND HUMAN RIGHTS ABUSES

GOVERNMENTS SHOULD ADOPT AND IMPLEMENT LAWS TO PROHIBIT ARMS EXPORTS UNLESS IT CAN BE DEMONSTRATED THEY WILL NOT CONTRIBUTE TO SERIOUS HUMAN RIGHTS VIOLATIONS, CRIMES AGAINST HUMANITY OR WAR CRIMES.

AMNESTY INTERNATIONAL

WWW.AMNESTYUSA.ORG

AMNESTY INTERNATIONAL

CELEBRATES THE 50TH ANNIVERSARY OF THE UNIVERSAL DECLARATION OF HUMAN RIGHTS. 1948-1998

Designer? It's the same thing to him. Indeed, some of graphic design's most famous precursors, such as Kurt Schwitters and Alexander Rodchenko, moved fluently between both worlds. The point was communication, not professionalization. But, over the course of a century pushed along by an explosion of commercial culture, professionalism won out. So by the time Woody entered the scene in the '60s, he had to make a choice. And he's quite candid in saying that it was his own fear of the art world that led him to design.

"I entered a field chosen by those who wanted to be artists and didn't want to take the risk of not making money. I didn't go to art school. I didn't do any of that stuff. My work is all about being a frustrated artist in a commercial world."

But artistic frustration has been conspicuously absent from Pirtle's work. Even at his first $500-a-month job, at Glenn Advertising in Dallas in the early '70s, he was aware that, however commercial and prosaic, design problems were, in fact, profound little puzzles of art and humanity. How can we make a person feel? How can we get a person to stop? How can we get a person to change? With the talent of a master illustrator and a rare gift for the bold gesture, Pirtle has unearthed essential truths buried beneath impenetrable client mission statements and mushy corporate-style specifications. Boiling things down and getting his own way in the design process has been a two-track strategy throughout his career, and he has little interest in deconstructing it. Pirtle is a designer who believes in magic as an explanation for his success. But it is the down-to-earth magic of the Texan conjurer who can lure a rattlesnake from the backseat of a Chevy while driving down the interstate.

"When I entered the business, I didn't have a sense of what you were supposed to do. I've always tried to blur the lines between the commercial and art world. Why is this any different than doing a painting? And the more I did, the more I realized that it really wasn't that different. And today I would really not think it is different at all. It's only a different way of

Top left: Identity for the Flying Fish Brewing Co., 1995.
Left: Identity for the film production company Fine Line Features, 1991. **Opposite:** *Poster for Amnesty International, 1998.*

Hot Seat

Knoll

delivering a product." Pirtle thinks broadly when he talks about product. A more satisfying word for his notion might be the abstract: outcome.

His early work with Glenn Advertising was informal, improvisational, not out of some ideology, but because it was more fun that way. He synthesized his clients' strategies and goals, but the work was all about waiting for inspiration amid organized play. Pirtle became art director almost immediately, when a colleague suddenly departed. Eventually Glenn Advertising became Bozell and Jacobs, and after a two-year stint there, he joined the Richards Group, when Stan Richards took Pirtle under his wing.

Stan Richards had a word to describe Woody. A word Woody didn't even know at the time. The word was "indefatigable." "I worked all the time. It wasn't uncommon for us to stay up all night three nights a week just because we loved it. You were doing what you loved doing."

For Pirtle, design went well beyond the limited vision of any single client, job, or teacher. Instead one finds in all of Pirtle's work a constant fiddling with the mix of private and public. Each job is a search for the balance between art and design, which, for Woody, is a personal struggle to understand the nature of creativity itself. It is a struggle involving some very personal demons. In the early days, Pirtle was betting everything on the next job, waiting for inspiration, sometimes daring it not to come.

"I would have some assignment, and I would go to bed the night before not having anything. I'd get up at four and work until seven, and then I would take a shower. I arranged it so it would have to happen between four and seven or else I was out of luck. But it always did."

Besides excelling at playing teenage games of chicken against his own mind, there were also valuable, more concrete lessons from those early days. For all the fun, there was a logic and a formality to his collaboration with Stan Richards that underpins all of Pirtle's work. "His whole methodology was concept, concept, concept. If you can outthink them you will always come out on top. If you come up with the right idea and find the best

Left: "Hot Seat" poster for Knoll furniture, 1980. **Opposite:** *Recruitment poster for the Ringling School of Art, 1992.*

156

RINGLING SCHOOL OF ART AND DESIGN   Bachelor of Fine Arts Degree and Certificate Programs in Computer Graphics, Fine Arts, Graphic Design, Illustration and Interior Design. For information, graphic arts, write or call Office of Admissions, 2700 North Tamiami Trail, Sarasota, Florida 34234   CALL (813) 351-4614 OR (800) 255-7695

way to implement it you'll be all right. Don't worry about style, don't worry about trends."

However, there was one trend that unquestionably helped the Dallas piece of Pirtle's career. The explosive growth of commerce and culture in the American Southwest during the '70s and '80s brought opportunities and a renewed interest in the region's distinctive imagery. One of Pirtle's early clients was the Texas-based T.G.I. Friday's. With money, and more important, the guts to try something new to take the tiny restaurant chain national, the partners gave Pirtle wide latitude and an environment of freedom. "These were some of the best working relationships I ever had. No focus groups." Pirtle's menu concept, a spiral-bound composition notebook with hand lettering, suggested both daring and nostalgia, that customers were back playing hooky from school. Apparently, they were as big a hit as the food. "People would walk out the door with the menus."

Early on his work evolved into a distinctive form of cultural anthropology, an outgrowth of being a keen observer of consumer behavior. Pirtle resisted focus groups because he preferred to watch the consumer in his natural habitat. Such techniques are a formalized aspect of many design practices today. For Pirtle it has always been informal, a consequence of being naturally sociable, with an artist's reverence for the artifacts of everyday life. He would loot and collect anything, and his net was thrown wide. He would prowl the junkyards and back roads of Dallas driving around in his own piece of hippie Americana, a VW bus. The things he collected were rarely of any immediate use, but the whole exercise became part of a deeper quest that would eventually define the mature designer he was becoming. What Pirtle found most satisfying about junkyards was that they gave him the chance to reveal the narrative of objects. Items thrown away acquired connotations and retained memories even as they lost their utility. Even more significant, random combinations of objects suggested relationships that were not obvious but still powerful and intuitive.

A lot of Pirtle's work involves finding the abrupt and uncommon union between symbols and making them work together. Collage became his favored medium (as, coincidentally, it was Schwitters's and Rodchenko's) because it allowed him to recontextualize found pictures and objects—in essence, to abstract them—without sacrificing their recognizability. Business cards pinned to a corkboard become an intimate biography of a complex personality. A jalapeño reclining over a pedestal becomes a Hot Seat for Knoll furniture. A discarded, and decidedly unappetizing, skeleton of a fish becomes a crudely sketched airplane and irresistible logo for Flying Fish Brewing Co. Pirtle's crunching together of stark contrasts engages curiosity and invites observers to

Above: Shopping bags for the American Folk Art Museum in New York, part of a new identity program timed to the museum's move into a new building, 2001. Opposite: Poster announcing the reopening of the American Folk Art Museum at the new location.

take a leap with him—a populist's strategy if there ever was one.

That challenge to take a leap comes from Pirtle's surprising concatenations and unexpected visual hyphenations and is a source of energy for people, driving them deeper into the images. It is about storytelling, and he is reluctant to say why this succeeds in the corporate world, but he feels that clients are often hungry to see things in a new way as long as they believe the designer understands their business, and their risks are minimized.

"They think you are getting paid well for immersion in their culture. When they think you have done that extremely well and put it into the hopper with everything else, you still have to come back to them with something that turns everything upside down, that puts it in a way that no one has ever thought of before."

It was long after he discovered he could be successful with clients that Pirtle began to embrace design as more of an integrated personal ethos.

In the 1980s he lost his seventeen-year-old son Mark in a car accident, killed while on a teenage road trip across the South. Pirtle learned of the death in a phone call to the Louisiana state police on Easter Sunday. The death was part of a chain of events that transformed Pirtle's life. Within a year Pirtle's marriage fell apart, and he himself was the victim of a serious pedestrian accident: A car struck him and practically tore him apart. Physical and mental recovery led to a reexamination of his priorities. Pirtle vowed to place whatever family he had left (he has twin daughters, Amy and Elizabeth) at the center of his life. Design now became a way of deciding how to live as well as a way of producing clever images for people far outside his emotional realm. In 1988 he became a Pentagram partner.

Pirtle remarried, and with his second wife, Leslie Pirtle, he has for more than fifteen years centered his work around a living space of his own design. The separation of home and workplace became blurred; inspiration and energy flowed continuously between the domestic and the public realms of his life. First, in a nineteenth-century farmhouse in Bridgehampton, New York, from which he would commute three days a week into Manhattan for Pentagram. Today, in a sprawling eighteenth-century property in upstate New York: a former industrial mill with residential buildings and a former tavern, all huddled along the river near the Hudson Valley town of New Paltz. It is both art studio for the no-longer-frustrated artist and a life project for Pirtle, his wife, and their eleven-year-old son, Luke.

With a newfound personal clarity Pirtle produced arguably his most important identity work for Fine Line Features, Champion Athletic products, Delta Faucet, Callaway Golf, Amnesty International, and

*Above: Donor wall constructed of found wooden planks for the American Folk Art Museum, 2001. **Opposite:** Illustration from a holiday campaign for booksellers Barnes & Noble, 2003.*

En Garde Arts. The symbols are classic simplicity, but they, like his found objects, tell a story.

Pirtle's lifelong passion for rummaging through junkyards has now been translated into a core design aesthetic: collage. His studio is filled with scraps and ephemera rife with potential. A stack of discarded architectural ornaments, blocks of carved wood, are stacked in an exploration of abstract vertical form. There is no specificity to the work, but Pirtle plays with the vertical in his studio until a piece begins to form, until the elements seem to belong together despite their contrasts, and then a practical idea tumbles out. He pulls from his desk a sketch for a Barnes & Noble holiday-campaign image: Stacked books perfectly referencing the studio piece are composed into a Christmas-tree pyramid capped with a bow. The vertical evokes the iconic tree and coins another icon, an architectural monument to the act of book buying. For Pirtle, this direct line from artist's studio to client presentation is a proud summation of his life's work.

These tangible, hands-on qualities of creation and destruction in art are exactly what Pirtle finds so lacking in the design profession today. His training came well before digital technology and in a swaggering tone of one who's mastered his craft, he claims to value his old skills more than ever.

"I always knew I could draw," he says. "I came up in the days of rubber cement and spray mount. I can draw Bodoni, every character, in several weights. I know Bodoni inside and out. Having that kind of skill is invaluable. Doing pasteups where you cut out every individual letter and space it. I can letterspace better than anybody here," referring to the young, sophisticated technological wizards who roam the cluttered corridors at Pentagram. It is a plea for authorship through craft, a plea that frames an increasingly visible debate in the design community at large, a realization that mastery of machines is not the same as self-mastery.

Pirtle bemoans the retreat of messiness from the studio even as young innovators attempt to reinvent digital tools to embody the traditional elements of craft, hands-on feedback, the physical intimacy of paper and glue. We're not there yet, according to Pirtle, who finds himself spending too much time waiting for things to print out. "I'll never outgrow that graphite mentality. I love using my hands. That's what I think I do best. I can create imagery with my hands."

Digital technology has at the very least rendered print media generic, given it a Walkman mentality, where everyone has headphones but few can actually play an instrument. Digital technology has created the myth that design is easy, part of the software loaded with your computer. This, Pirtle says, has direct consequences for the profession. It makes the case for design even harder.

Pirtle believes that the timeless qualities of good design are in danger of being drowned out by the chatter of the commercial world. Being willing to fight a battle to stay out of the background and be heard above the noise is the essential passion of any good designer. "I think at the end of the day what it's about is having your way. If you're going to be a designer, you are only a comma or a hue away from success and failure. It can be something as small as one number in the Pantone book, a punctuation mark away from getting it wrong." Woody Pirtle, at sixty, has been coaxing icons from noise for decades now. He fiddles with pieces of the puzzle, tweaks the story line, but the image in his mosaic is as sharp as it's ever been.

Look Right, Work Right

Bruce Sterling on *Robert Brunner*

ROBERT BRUNNER HAS HAD a more direct effect on my life and work than any other designer. This man designed the Apple Keyboard II. I pounded that keyboard relentlessly for years, writing novels, wrestling the muse, making the mortgage, and feeding the children.

Many a colleague of mine has fallen in the trenches, wrist tendons blown out from carpal tunnel syndrome, but although I type wondrously badly, I've never suffered that occupational illness. That's because the well-crafted keyboard of Robert Brunner's design was sparing me (and countless others) these gratuitous physical insults.

Robert Brunner was once the chief of the Apple Industrial Design group. Sometime after he left Apple, I dared to buy a PC, but I swiftly learned my lesson and gave it to my teenager. I can't work on a sorry contraption like that; I'm a serious artist. I write with Apples, and whenever I break them from overuse, I just buy more.

This keyboard is far from the only Brunner contribution to my well-being. There's also my toothbrush. Although he did not design it, it came from Lunar Design, an outfit that Brunner founded in 1984 for his moonlighting activities. Every day I check my schedule, too. It is scrawled on a big wall calendar, designed in Robert Brunner's San Francisco Pentagram office. There must be many other such influences—but these three confront me literally every day.

Robert Brunner now works at Pentagram, a design outfit so esteemed that they handle Pantone's brand identity—which would make Pentagram not just the designers' designers, but the designers' designers' designers. The Pentagram office in San Francisco is a former factory nestled amid apartment buildings and parking garages, a few blocks from the downtown arts district. This factory has been peeled out to the ducts, pipes, and exposed concrete, then retrofitted with sheet glass, aluminum, and blond wood. Its tall, sunlit loftspaces are punctuated by flights of perforated stairs that lead me to Brunner's wall-fronted office overlooking the street.

Brunner is a tall, soft-spoken, sandy-haired, forty-something Californian, the father of four.

Opposite: Dell Latitude Notebook, 2003.

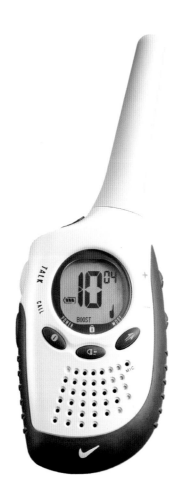

He has crinkly blue eyes, faded blue jeans, a sturdy long-sleeved shirt, and low-key but offbeat black walking shoes. Born in 1958 in San Jose, the heart of Silicon Valley, he has an innate feeling for gizmos and gadgets that few can rival. He is the son of a disk-drive engineer and literally a child of the computer industry.

The sturdy wall shelving behind his black Aeron chair sports some remarkable trophies. Nostalgia lances my heart at the welcome sight of an Apple PowerBook, once a treasured prop in my favorite author publicity photo. The shelf also features the "Mindset" IBM compatible (an instant MoMA trophy at the dawn of Brunner's career) plus the Mac LC and the Mac Color Classic, pop-hits for Apple on which Brunner once worked. Lower shelves carry a broad array of kid pics and a number of sailing mementos. Bob Brunner's cell phone plays the *Popeye the Sailor* theme song when it rings. He's a rather serious, muscular sailor who eats his spinach and likes to push the performance limits of the craft. His Hobie Cat has capsized so many times it's known as "This Side Up."

Brunner removes a bulky knick-knack from a lower shelf. This was one of his earliest efforts: a veterinary injector for cattle. Brunner deftly checks the hypodermic action on this gizmo, and, sturdy and dependable as ever, it gives off a firm, no-nonsense "whackety-CLACK!" It's not all consoles and joysticks for Bob, the creator of this handheld, drug-squirting shotgun for cows.

Then there is the Pentagram hammer. As Brunner points out, it makes little sense to "stuff some digital" into a mere hammer, a tool that exists to wallop the living daylights out of nails. However, a hammer can definitely benefit from a designer with a thorough knowledge of high-performance contemporary materials, gained from a career involving electronics, medicine, and sporting goods. The Brunner Pentagram hammer remake features a shiny, precisely curved claw; black, rubberlike padding strips; a squaring, beveled head; a very narrow metal neck; and a swollen, cozy, resilient, shockproof grip. This startling device bears the same resemblance

Left: Nike ACG wireless radio, 2000. **Opposite:** *XB31 Digital Projector for Hewlett-Packard, 2003.*

to a commonplace wooden hammer that the Lunar Design Oral-B toothbrush does to a commonplace toothbrush, which is to say that the Pentagram hammer is a very Grand Vizier among hammers, a hammer that makes you wonder why mankind has been mucking about with inferior, low-tech hammers for the past forty thousand years.

Hammers, Brunner allows dryly, are "so much fun," but his services are more commonly sought by the high-tech likes of Dell and HP. Hence the new MP3 players he's worked on—not "shrunken Walkmans" but hand-friendly, digital-music devices.

Properly understood, an industrial product is not a static commodity packed in shrink wrap and styro blocks but a little drama. Brunner's job is to orchestrate this process and raise it to the heights of achievement. First comes the primal effort just to get the thing to work. To make it, in his term, "usable." There's many a conflict and sacrifice here, and a lot of them are not mechanical or engineering difficulties, but organizational ones. There are questions of internal corporate politics in the creation of products. Like, for instance, the very sharp differences between an exciting "challenge" (the goofy, half-baked idea that the client's technicians love because they made it up) and a "problem" (the unfortunate label slapped on a good idea by clients suffering from Not Invented Here syndrome). Here's where a designer's professional judgment comes in handy.

Many newfangled devices that do become "usable" do not succeed, because they're just not "useful." They can be used for something, but the thing they do is not something that real people want done in their real lives.

The third and highest tier is neither the "usable" nor the "useful," but the "desirable." When desire occurs, a device has kindled a kind of romance with the user. It has engaged them emotionally. When a product has a lively, well-considered awareness of user needs and customer intentions, it becomes deeply satisfying, like a well-told story. And, since it knowingly exploits continuing, basic improvements in material technology, a well-designed product is

Right: Stowaway portable keyboard for Think Outside, 1999.
Opposite: Fuego Ultimate BBQ for Design Within Reach, 2003.

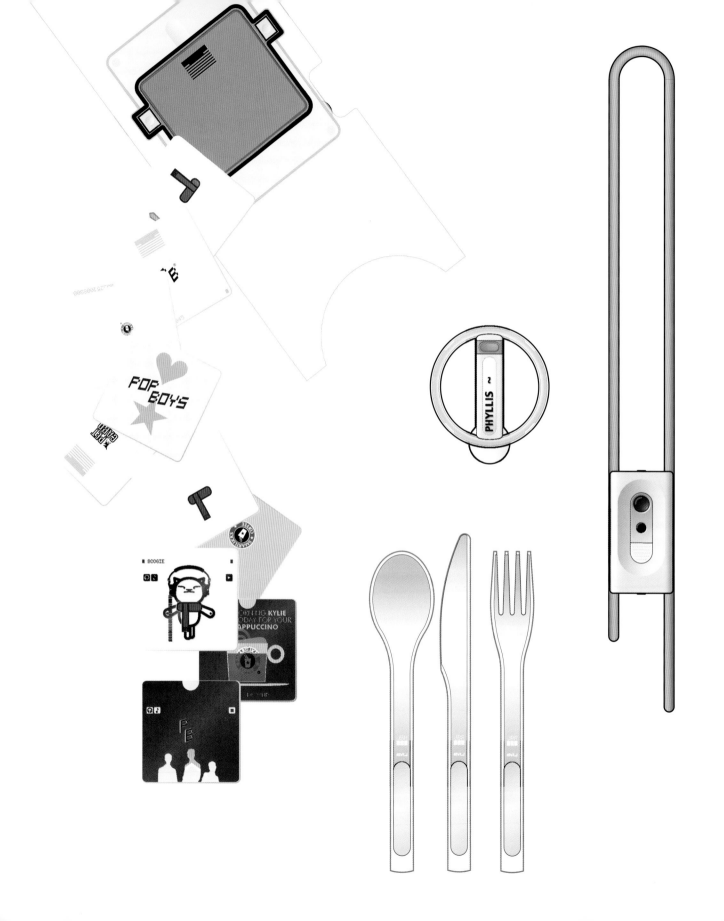

a progressive story, a product that seems to lean forward into futurity. Not only do you desire it—you desire everything else to become like it.

In the period 1990–96, Brunner's Apple Industrial Design group won more design awards than the rest of the computer industry combined. These were devices whose physicality and form predicted what was coming, not just for Silicon Valley and its legions of geeks, hackers, and overachievers, but for society generally and globally. They were signature devices of their times, in much the way that the streamlined trains of Dreyfuss and Loewy defined the 1930s.

Now, Brunner muses, a generation of digital connoisseurs have grown up surrounded by such machines. Consumers are no longer fascinated by computers per se. They are no longer impressed by all of the many vaguely "usable" things that the machine can do, as the cheap-and-easy dazzlement of a million menu choices wears off quickly. Computers are plenty powerful now, so people no longer think in basic engineering terms of RAM or ROM. Today, they prize the "useful."

Hence a new world of digital convergence has emerged in products, like the "camera-phone." Despite its hybrid name, a camera-phone is not merely a phone combined with a camera. If you jam a phone and camera into the same chassis, you create a clumsy hybrid that does neither job well. A good camera-phone would be better understood as a convergence of useful functions: a handheld digital platform that can create graphic files and move them wirelessly. How do you make that device desirable? Make the convergence simple: intuitive and fingertip-quick. The two virtues—Convergence and Simplicity—pull in two different directions, they quarrel with each other, they are forced to a harsh give and take, but they are the parents of good products.

Consumer items need emotional content, the ability to establish a lasting relationship with the user. And they do that. I have certainly spent many thousands of hours with various Apple machines, far more than I ever do with my household cats.

---

*Opposite: Concepts for the Connected Network, a project for AT&T exploring the possibilities presented by broadband wireless technologies, 2001. **Right:** Nike Typhoon watch, 1999.*

They're mere machines, but it is hard to miss the sophistication of the design language there. The shapes are expressive. Macs and PowerBooks can be recognized instantly. As sculptured objects, they deftly mix simple surfaces with complex, fluted, and perforated ones. They are complicated devices that invite yet do not overwhelm. The sheen of the light changes at different angles, with metals and plastics mixing gloss and matte. And wherever the thing is to be stroked, prodded, pounded, clicked, or caressed, there is always some subtle hint, some extra bit of detailing, some act of friendliness that tells us that somebody out there knows that we have fingers and thumbs.

Brunner now rises from his Aeron to go on a gizmo search. As a science-fiction writer, this is definitely the high point of my visit—we're going down to the basement, to the place where Pentagram keeps the stuff that doesn't work yet.

Front and center is the Pentagram/Design Within Reach digital barbecue. This gleaming prototype is not scheduled for production—it's a prop for a TV documentary. A techno-gourmand vista of hardwood, slate, and sheet steel, it could probably be made to exist, using current technology, for something in the neighborhood of five thousand dollars.

More interesting is the question of why anyone would want to "stuff some digital" into a patio barbecue (complete with handheld remote control). The answer is: The thing just cooks better. Lots better. It's loaded with sensors and auto-adjusts: The grills creep silently up and down as the coals grow hotter and colder. It's a barbecue that senses what the fire is doing and how the food is reacting to it.

On the walls are foam board posters with some blue-sky Pentagram notions. One of them muses on what might happen if the Pokemon-style craze for children's collectible cards was replaced with collectible children's "smart cards" that could read and carry data from child to child. Another forecasts a digitally redesigned intensive-care hospital environment where the digitized knives and forks can tell nurses if the patient is eating, and what the patient liked best, and how much of the food he ate, and how long it took him to eat it.

It may seem rather out-there and whimsical to "stuff some digital" into a handheld fork, especially when they are depicted as ultracheap, antiseptic, and disposable. But just how far-fetched is that idea, really?

It wasn't long ago when people wondered why anyone would ever put a computer chip into a mere handheld doorknob. I'm in a hotel right now, and this hotel still uses brass keys with mechanical locks. These brass keys seem distinctly hazardous, time-consuming, and primitive to me now. What if I lose my key? What if some crook copies it? Hotel doors all over the planet have been stuffed with digital.

The project keeping Brunner happy at the moment is golf clubs. He knows little or nothing about them. That's why he likes the assignment. He waxes joyfully about the golf-ball-testing laboratory he just witnessed, where giant spinning wheels impart hooks and slices to flying golf balls under ultracontrolled lab conditions, as a host of high-speed digital videocams tracks the airborne ball behavior. "It's a full-scale NASA-style setup there," he grins. Brunner is not simply going to redesign golf clubs, for the task at hand is not a product but a product line: an integrated set of golf clubs that require associated design elements, so that they will fit together in the bag as a neat cluster. The clubs will need some graphic unity inside that bag, a design strategy, not coincidentally, that will work wonders for branding.

As I leave, I ask Bob Brunner what it is that people most need to know about him. His answer is immediate: He's a guy who "wants things to look right and work right." Even back in high school, he made it his goal to have the best-looking tool kit in shop class. His beautiful toolbox quickly fell apart, though, because he hadn't yet learned anything about real-world engineering.

Industrial design turned out to be the fulfillment of the dream of his youth: Brunner is still that imaginative Silicon Valley kid who wanted it to look right and work right. But now, as a Pentagram partner with a dizzying variety of projects under his belt, he's precisely the kind of guy who can make that happen in the real world.

Opposite: Heavy Hitter hammer, 2000.

The Customer
Is Always Wrong

Stephen Bayley on *David Hillman*

IN THE WEEK OF HIS SIXTIETH BIRTHDAY David Hillman leaned across the table, and I looked him in his twinkling eye. I was asking what he had learnt in his time as a professional designer. Without flinching or hesitation Hillman said: "It's easy. The client is never right." Oh, that's very interesting, I thought. Combative but good, nonetheless, to know where you stand. It's pleasantly refreshing to get a bit of honesty on these occasions. Especially as, on this particular occasion, Hillman's the client and I am the consultant. "But," I said, referring to one of Hillman's most attractive recent jobs where a tired-looking product was dramatically energized with his characteristic style, "what about so-and-so? He seems okay?" It took Hillman a moment to make his judgment, and then he said, "Totally fucking obnoxious."

Hillman comes from a generation born before television created a global monoculture, although he is of an age that made him alert to its impending possibilities. He was, for instance, twelve years old when British television broadcast its first-ever advertisement (for toothpaste). In addition, his father worked for Pathé, the cinema news supplier. So from childhood Hillman was aware of how images are captured and conveyed. And sold. With more characteristic candor Hillman explained that this family introduction to the media had the additional happy advantage of meaning he never had to pay to go to the movies.

As a student at the London School of Printing before "graphic design" existed, Hillman was in a position to witness an important episode in the professionalizing of design: In those days graphics was called commercial art, although it was Hillman's tutor Tom Eckersley who later coined the neologism that stuck. But before that coinage Eckersley merely drew a notional line down the studio floor between typographers and illustrators. Hillman found himself with the typographers, and the traditional disciplines and craft he learnt at the tough school of the LSP—fonts, weights, kerning—have been with him ever since.

Hillman began work as London entered the '60s: Among the many distinctions of this crucial decade was an explosion of the media. The sensibilities of

Opposite: 1991/92 catalog for Phaidon Press, part of design program including a new mark, book covers, and catalogs, 1991.

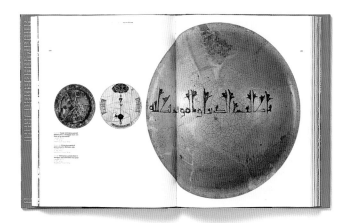

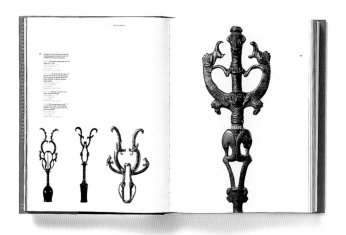

the world of advertising, with its big budgets and high production values and glossy finish and slick patter, made traditional culture look dull and slow. And the new media had the technology too. This was a world of Hasselblads and Arriflex and Miller-geared heads.

This was the world of *The Sunday Times Magazine*, which Hillman joined as a design assistant. Impossible to believe today, but forty years ago *The Sunday Times* and its revolutionary "colour supplement" was the great taste-making and opinion-forming vehicle of its day. Here the cooks, novelists, fashion designers, and rock stars who animated the new London were presented—in striking layouts using grain and bleed—to a curious, blinking nation only just emerging from an age of rationing.

From design assistant Hillman graduated to edit *The Sunday Times Magazine*'s environment section (in the days when "environment" was a radical proposition) while working on a redesign of the entire newspaper. Occupying a focal position in British popular culture was no bad place for an ambitious designer. At one time or another everyone who was anyone (and a lot who were neither) passed through the ever-expanding pages of *The Sunday Times*. Hillman had Man Ray photograph Catherine Deneuve for the magazine cover. Thus the artistic highs and revelatory eroticism of '60s culture were neatly bracketed. I asked Hillman what it was like, using one of the world's greatest-ever photographers and one of the world's most beautiful women on a throwaway. He said, "These were just people—like David Hockney and Peter Blake—you worked with." "What did you pay him?" I asked. "Man Ray got page rates, just like anybody else." An amazing school of high art and hard noses, but Hillman left *The Sunday Times* because "it got too easy."

This was 1970, the year of the White Album. Hillman was appointed art director of *Nova*, a monthly magazine with a sharp profile and sky-high production values. During that stint, he assumed the responsibilities of deputy editor as well. Unusually, these dual responsibilities gave him exceptional control over the character and appearance of the

Opposite and right: Splendour of Iran, *a collection of three volumes designed for Booth-Clibborn Editions, 2001.*

magyar. Certainly *The Sunday Times Magazine* had been very influential, but as a give-away supplement to an already successful newspaper it had never been tested in the market. *Nova* was different. Here was an opportunity to use the very best art, design, photography, and writing and see if it would sell. It was a taste test for the British consumer. "I had a very strong idea of what it should be. I had done it before," Hillman told me.

*Above: Signage program for the National Maritime Museum in Greenwich, London, 1999. **Opposite:** Millennium Stamps series for the Royal Mail, 1999.*

And *Nova* made a very strong impression indeed. Typography was used to make an exceptional impact. Hillman was uncompromising in using the best photographers: Like Man Ray at *The Sunday Times*, Helmut Newton worked for *Nova*. Issey Miyake's first collection was published here. The mood of 1971 was precarious and significant for Britain: National icon Rolls-Royce went bust with a fixed-price contract to supply Lockheed with RB-211 turbofans for its L-1011 airplanes[1]; the currency went decimal; the Open University was founded; and three classic British movies were aired: *A Clockwork Orange*, *Death in Venice*, and *Sunday*

Bloody Sunday. So in these larger auguries was a picture of a changing nation: old institutions going into ruin while new ones emerged, and a sharp new-media consciousness rubbing along with the eroticization of almost everything...including an ad for Fison's pharmaceuticals in the then-staid *Times* that had a nude model. This was not a soft-focus image but a handsome woman with prominently erect nipples.

Nova picked up all these elements and was both sexy and sexual. The very best of '70 sensibility (as cool as the '60, but more mature and professional) was captured by Hillman's magazine, never more so than in November 1971. For this edition Hillman engineered a classic of journalism when the photographer Harri Peccinotti was sent out with a bunch of five-pound notes and asked girls he found on the street to lift their shirt and (if wearing one) to remove their bra and have themselves featured in Britain's cleverest (and sexiest) magazine. They did. They were. And everyone who saw it will never forget. In all its Jack the Lad cockiness, this one feature was a signature of Hillman's style: A smart idea and an irreverent attitude to the consumer (nudity was then rare) were resolved and commercialized by fastidious typography and layout into a brilliant result. This masterpiece of magazine art pointed to a future where slick sexuality became a familiar working tool.

In 1975 Hillman left *Nova* and started his own business, this time not because it was getting too easy, but because *Nova* was just a little ahead of its time and short-lived. There was an expectation that Hillman would become a fashion photographer, but he says he found the actual camera work boring. "I'm at my happiest looking at photographs, riffling through a million negatives and just trying to distil the essence for a feature." So he stayed in newspapers and magazines, designing Paris's *Le Matin* before joining Pentagram in 1978. At Pentagram Hillman had the opportunity to apply a successful art director's sensibility to a big corporate identity job. It was a unique opportunity and a unique environment.

Right: Cover and spreads from Terence Donovan: The Photographs, *published by Little Brown & Company, 2001.*
Opposite: Editing process for the Terence Donovan book.

Terence
Donovan

At Pentagram no one specializes. "You join this group and you learn," Hillman explained. "I'd think twice about designing a house, but on the other hand there's so much expertise around here, I'd probably end up doing it." So in this spirit, never having done a corporate identity before, Hillman set about Skandia, a giant Swedish insurance, pensions, and savings organization. Founded in 1855, Skandia had a unique business philosophy, accepting clients only by personal recommendation: Thus with neither salesmen nor tied agents, the business can be both flexible and moral. Since Hillman insists, "I have to feel good about what I'm doing," this was an appropriate start. Clients may not always be right, but some are less wrong than others.

The 1988 redesign of *The Guardian* is Hillman's signature. I said to him that, being fresh and clear and optimistic, it has got all the elements of your personal style, but he replied that he was skeptical about any particular handwriting, suggesting that all there is in common with other projects is a shared thought

process. Still, like *The Sunday Times*, *The Guardian* was a British institution that needed, as Terry Southern once described the editing process, "brightening and tightening." But *The Guardian* was of a very different type to *The Sunday Times*. It is owned by the Scott Trust, a Mancunian nonconformist charity, like Skandia, with a strong moral tone and left bias, the favorite read of armchair radicals, students, schoolteachers, and other public-sector employees. Paradoxically this is a conservative audience in matters of taste and Hillman innovated: For the first time a daily British newspaper had a mixed font title and appeared in two sections, based on a clearly articulated grid.

These simple devices revolutionized the appearance of British broadsheet newspapers: Suddenly all

---

Above: Identity and packaging for Wistbray's range of Dragonfly Naturally Caffeine Free Rooibos teas, 2003.
Opposite: Identity and packaging for Wistbray's range of Dragonfly Organic teas, 2000.

The Guardian's competitors looked as though they belonged—as they did—to the generation before. The mixed-font title was typical of Hillman in that it was based on traditional typographer's perceptions but adopted and directed to a modern end. At the London School of Printing Hillman was taught that type was a functional tool, not a decorative device. The mixture of faces used on *The Guardian* expressed with quiet energy and elegant subtlety the newspaper's ethos: looking forward and backward at the same time, modern but respectful of tradition. This thoughtful but unforced use of the tools of his craft is exactly the same as Elmore Leonard's approach to his own work: "If it sounds like writing, I rewrite it." Just change the word "writing" for "design" and you have the same thing.

So what of David Hillman the person? Ask him has favorite places and he says San Francisco, New York, and Australia ("It's fresh, no hang-ups"). But now this quintessential Londoner lives in Gloucestershire. He's a relaxed man, tanned and fit from cycling, but he really does have this thing about clients. "I refuse to be treated as a supplier," he says. "I am more than that. I know exactly what I'm doing. And they don't. Let's face it, if a client really knew what he wanted he wouldn't come to anybody else to solve his problems. The successful jobs are based on equal partnerships, living off each other's experiences." Good. Combative stuff, but I want to know if in the end it is an art or a science. Hillman confesses to an element of cussed creative whim: "Yeah sure," he says—but then looks doubtful. I don't believe he thinks it matters what it's called so long as it works. "I see someone reading *The Guardian*," he says, "and I still feel good about it. You do a piece of packaging that has been successful: That's great. That's the reason for doing what we do. If I weren't interested in making other people's products successful, I'd be a painter."

Hillman sits with a big piece of paper, solving problems. "That's the thing about being a commercial artist. You know, that's what we are! We're in the business of helping the client shift his goods." More stirring realism. Where David Hillman came from they spoke about fifteen minutes of fame. Hillman has had at least half an hour...and there's more to come. But only for the right sort of client.

1. The downfall of Rolls-Royce was momentous in the history of British self-regard. The aero-engine company (that emerged from the car manufacturer: They are now separate because of the events I describe) was the lofty pinnacle of British technology. Rolls-Royce was so anxious to get on board the US wide-body aerial bandwagon in the late '60 (which produced the 747, DC-10, and L-1011) that they offered Lockheed a fixed-price contract to supply engines for the L-1011 (or Tristar). Development was more costly than anticipated, and Rolls- Royce went bust.

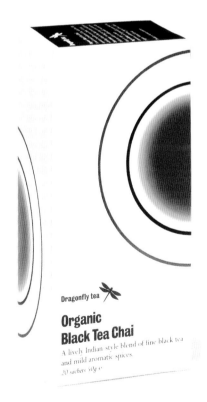

Dragonfly tea

Organic Black Tea Chai

A lively Indian style blend of fine black tea and mild aromatic spices.
20 sachets 50g e

Hunter Gatherer

Owen Edwards on *Kit Hinrichs*

EVERY LIFE HAS A TIPPING POINT, a moment when a kid's response to the standard question "What do you want to be when you grow up?" changes from cowboy, fireman, or nurse to electrical engineer, surgeon, or ichthyologist (though some do, of course, become cowboys, firefighters, or nurses). For Kit Hinrichs, this tipping point came one afternoon during his high-school years in the late '50s when he was helping his father clean out the family's garage in the San Fernando Valley town of North Hollywood. The improbable catalyst for Kit's life-changing moment was a pamphlet published by the US government on commercial art as a career, offering the astonishing revelation that a commercial artist might make as much as twenty-five dollars for a single drawing. In the commercial-art illustration of this moment, we see the lightbulb appear over Kit's head, with its radiating lines indicating ignition. Now, courtesy of the government printing office, Kit saw the future. For a teenager, the idea that money can be made by doing what you like to do anyway is perilously close to a miracle.

Once the idea of art as a living had taken hold, the luck of location came into play. Not far from Kit's family's home (not far by LA standards) was Art Center, considered by some the West Point of design schools, founded by Edward "Tink" Adams, and the alma mater of design pioneers from Lou Danziger to J Mays. What began there is the story of both a profession and a boy coming of age.

Kit's particular rite of passage, launched at Art Center, moved from the academy to the wider world when he took a year off from school and went to West Germany to serve as a volunteer at a boys' youth home in Mainz. He was there as a well intended person, not as a nascent designer. But the sojourn, and a bicycle trip through Italy he took while there, revealed to him a world where things looked entirely unlike what he had seen in Southern California. Modern devices—from cars to coffee makers—sprang from a sensibility that until then he had encountered only in the classroom. His was the kind of new Grand Tour that thousands of young Americans were making during these years, less to visit the classical ruins that young aristocrats

Opposite: Examples from Hinrichs's expansive American flag collection featured in the book Long May She Wave, *2001.*

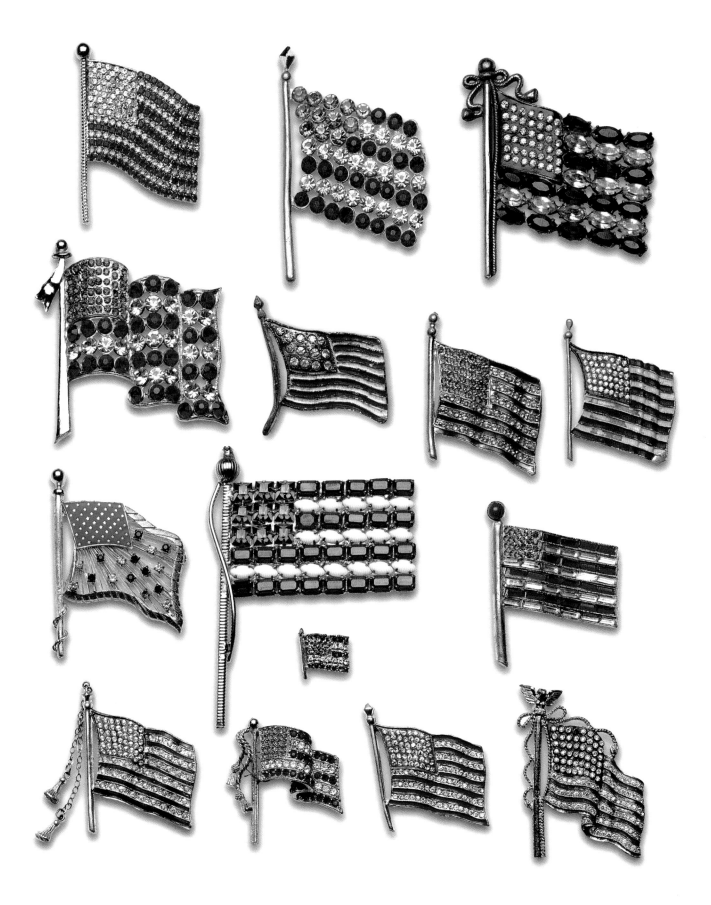

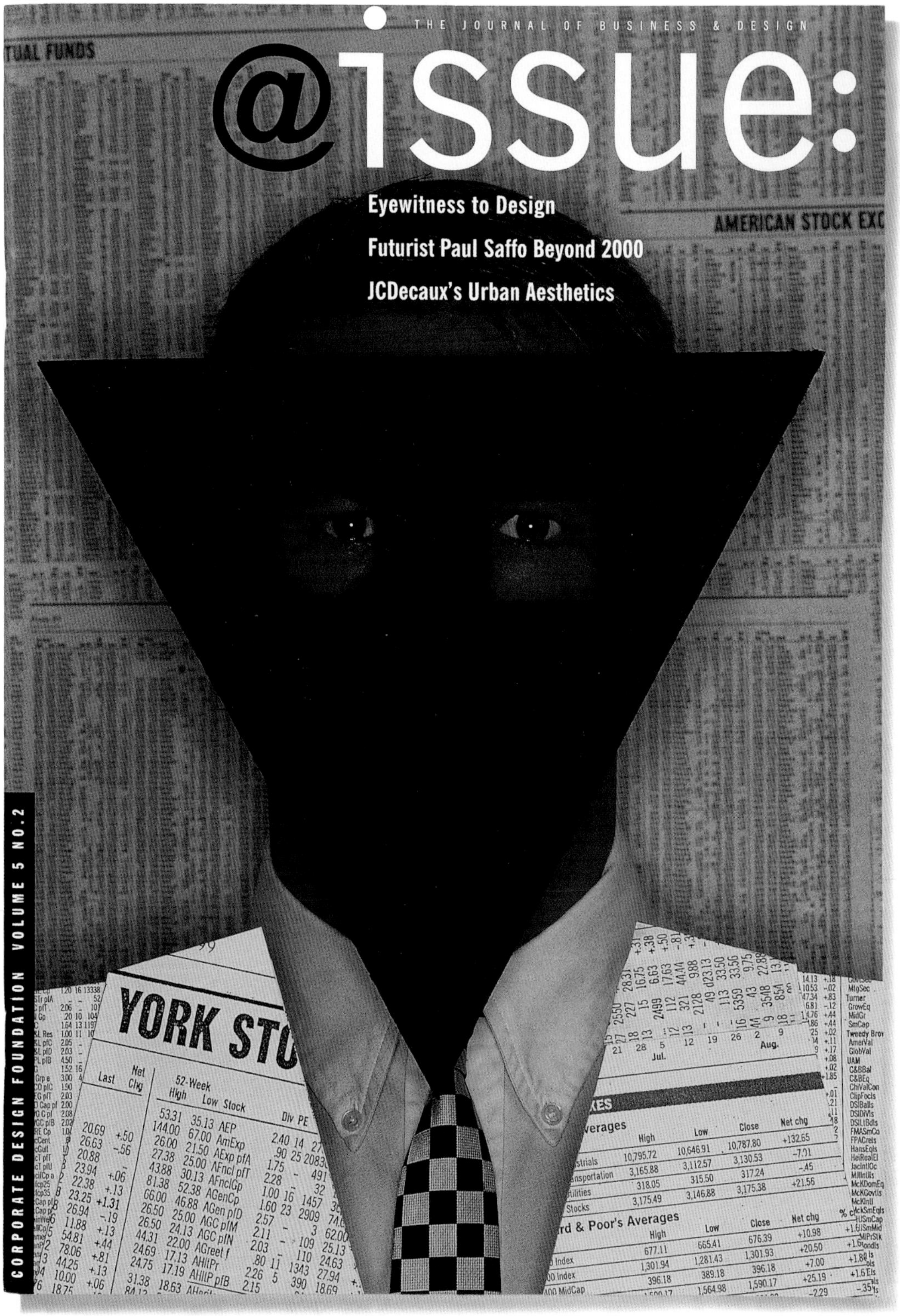

THE JOURNAL OF BUSINESS & DESIGN

@issue:

Eyewitness to Design

Futurist Paul Saffo Beyond 2000

JCDecaux's Urban Aesthetics

CORPORATE DESIGN FOUNDATION VOLUME 5 NO.2

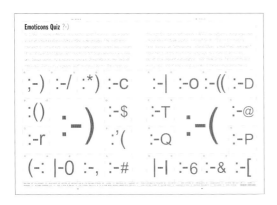

Left: Quiz spreads from @issue *magazine, 1997–present.*
Opposite: @issue *magazine cover, 1999.*

before the war had favored than to sit in the piazzas and browse through the ateliers of Europe.

Among his design heroes, along with renowned figures as Paul Rand and Pentagram London's Alan Fletcher and Colin Forbes, he names Willy Fleckhaus, the brilliantly innovative art director of *Twen* magazine in Germany. It's very possible that Kit encountered the high graphic energy of *Twen*'s pages during his year in Mainz. Influences blend into the transformative vision of any creative mind like streams feeding into a river and cannot easily be labeled, but it's safe to say that Italy and Germany, and the visionary likes of Fleckhaus, had no less effect on Kit than Art Center itself.

The combination of curiosity and altruism that took Kit to Europe mirrored the spirit of the late '50s and early '60s in the US, a period powered by the dual propulsive engines of optimism and discovery. Kit was part of the buoyant culture of the West Coast, seemingly limitless in its promise for a dazzling future. His father worked at Warner Brothers pictures as a soundman and sometimes on Saturdays, he would let Kit spend the day with him on movie sets in Burbank. There Kit watched the hopes of America shaped by Hollywood's formidable dream machine, and began to understand the power of visual persuasion.

Kit graduated from Art Center in 1963 on a Friday and on Saturday was standing at attention in San Diego. He had enlisted in the Marine Corps, a branch of the military well known for rigor and no less notable for its attention to physical appearances—in other words, the military branch most likely to appeal to a young designer. (Uniforms are custom-tailored to adjust to the rapidly changing physiques of recruits in training. In that respect, Kit says it was like working for Armani.) After a six-month tour of active duty, Kit made a fateful move to New York. For those lucky enough to have lived there at the time, the Apple was the sweetest of fruits, so tempting that a prudent soul might have been inclined to look around for a proffering serpent. As the grace of Europe had widened Kit's eyes, the grandeur of New York's soaring towers dazzled a kid reared in the ranch-house townscapes of the San Fernando Valley.

This was a time when even the most worldly New Yorkers were daily thrust into a whirlwind of sensation. It was as if bits of Europe had been brought home in the luggage of the newly itinerant Americans to be assembled into a kaleidoscope of revelation. Films by Bergman, Truffaut, Fellini, and Godard were changing the way we looked at movies (just think of those electrifying stop frames of Jeanne Moreau in *Jules et Jim*). Rerun film houses like the Thalia and the Eighth Street Playhouse served up a daily menu of compelling cinema, from classics to cult favorites. Woody Allen was doing stand-up comedy at the Village Vanguard. Jazz clubs like the Cookery and Basin St. East regularly featured such greats as Maynard Ferguson, Miles Davis, and Nina Simone. All of this energy overflowed into Madison Avenue, galvanizing advertising, magazines, and design.

The matter of innateness and influence—the nature-versus-nurture thing—is a complex cocktail; once stirred (or shaken), it's impossible to measure the ingredients. But it's a safe assumption that Kit's early years in the grip of this revolutionary ferment turned a curious young man into a voracious autodidact. With the skills he'd acquired at Art Center, he might have gone in any direction, but graphic design—essentially, at the time, ink on paper—was the right match for someone who was restlessly determined to learn new things. In fact, it was the very evanescence of graphic design that made the field appealing, since he could do so much more of it than, say, industrial design. It certainly didn't hurt that Kit found himself in a mother lode of design talent. He remembers going to an AIGA meeting and seeing, in one room, the most influential people in every aspect of graphic design. "I was like some young Catholic priest from Wichita," he says, "finding himself at the Vatican." He worked at various levels for various design studios, then teamed up with Anthony Russell to form Russell and Hinrichs, an independent design consultancy. By this time, Kit had earned his MA—Manhattan Assurance.

Tony Russell and Kit were partners for seven years—a seminal time, when Kit's signature approach to design began to gel. With scant resources he drew, he designed, he even staged photo shoots, serving as the model himself if need be, for clients that ranged from Sterling Drug to Chase Manhattan Bank. In short, he marshaled all the resources at his disposal. When the partnership dissolved, he and his wife, Linda Hinrichs, established Hinrichs Design Associates. Together they took on the task of rethinking the annual report. Instead of focusing strictly on the numbers and the organizational charts, they turned the genre into a vehicle for telling stories. In the process, they exponentially increased their profile as designers with commissions from Fortune 500 companies like Warner Communications. At the same time, they were the first wave of pioneers to set up house in Park Slope. Even the location of their office in the Flatiron district was prescient.

In 1976, the shifting winds of the economy, combined with the tug of family on the West Coast, led to Kit's departure from New York and his return to California with Linda. Together they helped form Jonson, Pedersen, Hinrichs & Shakery, modeled on and later to merge with Pentagram (an event that made Linda the firm's first female partner, from 1986 to 1993). Showing an early affinity for constructing professional bridges, they created the first bicoastal design partnership. Kit quickly discovered that San Francisco designers weren't interested in corporate work, leaving the field wide open to build a client list that included Crocker Bank, Transamerica, and Potlatch (for whom he has now designed over twenty-two annual reports). Potlatch is a case study in Kit's brand of narrative design. A typical annual report might feature the history of the pine tree and the history of building in the US, or the importance of water in growing trees and, ultimately, Potlatch profits. True to form, he did it drawing on an encyclopedic set of references, ranging from seventeenth-century engravings to Forestry Service materials to the endless ephemera in the company's archives.

The designer determined to keep all options open, to use anything and everything at hand, is someone who, like a novelist, knows that nothing learned or experienced ever goes to waste. Kit talks about

Opposite: Classic Typographic Calendar cover and pages, 2004.

365

August

1	2	3	4	5	6	7
8	9	10	11	12	13	14
15	16	17	18	19	20	21
22	23	24	25	26	27	28
29	30	31				

January

				1	2	3
4	5	6	7	8	9	10
11	12	13	14	15	16	17
18	19	20	21	22	23	24
25	26	27	28	29	30	31

October

					1	2
3	4	5	6	7	8	9
10	11	12	13	14	15	16
17	18	19	20	21	22	23
24/31	25	26	27	28	29	30

February

1	2	3	4	5	6	7
8	9	10	11	12	13	14
15	16	17	18	19	20	21
22/29	23	24	25	26	27	28

November

	1	2	3	4	5	6
7	8	9	10	11	12	13
14	15	16	17	18	19	20
21	22	23	24	25	26	27
28	29	30				

June

		1	2	3	4	5
6	7	8	9	10	11	12
13	14	15	16	17	18	19
20	21	22	23	24	25	26
27	28	29	30			

December

		1	2	3	4	
5	6	7	8	9	10	11
12	13	14	15	16	17	18
19	20	21	22	23	24	25
26	27	28	29	30	31	

GALACTIC CHOCOLATE SWIRL
All Natural Flavors

NEW YORK STRAWBERRY CHEESECAKE
All Natural Flavors

GRANDMA'S COOKIE JAR

CUPPA JOE
All Natural Flavors

VANILLA
All Natural Flavors

CHOCOLATE PEANUT BUTTER CHUNK
All Natural Flavors

HOT CHILLY CHILI
All Natural Flavors

BLUE RIBBON BERRY PIE
All Natural Flavors

CASHEW PRALINE PARFAIT
All Natural Flavors

BLACK RASPBERRY AVALANCHE
All Natural Flavors

CARAMEL TOFFEE BAR HEAVEN
Natural and Artificial Flavors Added

NUTS ABOUT MALT
Natural and Artificial Flavors Added

creating "time bridges" that constantly connect his past lives with his present work. Everything—his Boy Scout merit badges, old *Popular Mechanics* magazines that he read as a kid with their "little columns of stuff," even the King James Bible "red letter" edition with important passages in red—comes into play today. "Forty-five years after looking at that Bible," he says, "I'm still doing red captions. There's a bridge for me in these things."

This impulse to create connections—call it the collating imperative—is a direct reflection of his instincts as a collector; it is the design premise upon which his work rests. By virtue of his astonishing aggregation of American-flag memorabilia—the subject of his book *Long May She Wave*—Kit is a collector of considerable renown. What appeals to him is to take a theme—the flag, for example, or the myriad representations of the human face and form—and somehow make sense of an amazing spectrum of interpretations. "One of the reasons I love folk art," he says, "is that I'm always fascinated by how many variations others bring to a basic idea. When a thousand people interpret the theme of, say, the American flag, how can you not be fascinated?" Jostling for space on the shelves behind his desk at Pentagram's San Francisco office is a motley crowd of rubber dolls, carved figures, superheroes—rank after rank of homunculi Kit has come upon in flea markets, toy stores, and yard sales all over the world. Yet what might be an inchoate mob takes on a kind of ad hoc order in the connections Kit has managed to see among them, the felicitous happenstance of how one object relates to and animates another.

When Kit created *Review*, a magazine published by Art Center in the '90s, a regular feature in each issue was a pencil as imagined by a major designer, architect, or illustrator. In this same way, Kit's delight in variations on a theme and his pleasure in divining connections bring a rare combination of cohesion and serendipity to his designs. Not for nothing is he considered a master of the tabletop narrative.

Kit's insatiable curiosity about everything and anything accounts for the strong hint of a backstory informing all the elements on a Hinrichs-designed

Opposite: Naming, brand identity, and "dreamscape" images for Dreamery, a range of premium ice cream for Dreyers, 1998.

page. His favorite kind of narrative bridge is one that lets him cross the ravine between what he already knows and what he doesn't know yet.

It is possible, as a result of Kit's pleasure at finding things out, that a client may get more than was originally asked. Those who come to Kit specifically for an approach they've seen in his other work may be surprised to find that something about their particular message—something he may have never heard before—has taken him in an entirely surprising direction. Though Kit has a signal look—clear, orderly, energetic—that attracts new clients, he consistently avoids imitating (and boring) himself, imaginatively sidestepping the pitfalls of predictability. As is the case with other creative designers, this sometimes requires Kit to convince clients that what they are actually seeing is truer to their message than what they might have been expecting to see.

And there's no part of a Hinrichs plan that he won't have worked out down to the finest details. For instance, like many designers, Kit finds typefaces powerfully appealing (an appeal most publicly expressed by Pentagram's annual calendar celebrating typefaces and their inventors, one of his pet projects). But Kit is more than just a connoisseur of fonts; related to his affinity for type is an equal enthusiasm for print and knowledge of the printer's craft—an expertise owed to the ever-rarer generational advantage of having practiced on both sides of the digital divide.

In the best tradition of his heroes, Kit designs from the inside out—*his* inside, the hunter-gatherer's inside—rather than from the outside in. His approach is intelligent but not coolly intellectual, personal, not theoretical. This gives him a genial, we're-all-in-this-together kind of confidence that tells a client everything is going to be all right, the kind of reassuring bedside manner that doctors don't have the time for anymore. It is the job of any graphic designer, of course, to bring order out of a sack full of odd bits and of chaos, or at least to make some kind of two-dimensional sense out of pieces. But Kit brings something beyond that: a salve for anxiety.

Launching a new magazine is not a matter of life and death, of course. It just seems that way, especially to editors who think they have a good idea

but aren't entirely sure. Half the battle for an anxious editor—actually, more than half—is to be able to launch a magazine that *looks* like a magazine. As a developer of magazines myself, I have been a client of Kit's twice. As clients often are, I was faced with tight deadlines, a demanding publisher, and a few typed pages of optimistic but as yet unfulfilled assignments. In both cases, I was not at all sure of a good outcome.

When my colleagues and I stepped for the first time into the conference room at Pentagram in San Francisco and Kit walked in, sat down, and started to listen, I had a palpable feeling of relief: Here was someone who would see to it that things turned out okay. Kit has been described as "soft spoken, but clear about where he's headed, even extremely controlling with clients." That may not suit everyone, but at that worrisome moment, it worked for me. Forget about Kit as a young priest from Wichita—for me, the image was of a calm, confident marine who knew exactly what had to be done. So we went away, and I, for one, stopped worrying.

Left: New identity for the Museum of Glass: International Center for Contemporary Art, Tacoma, Washington, 2002.
Opposite: *Hall of Flags installation and signage system for the Museum of Glass.*

Our House
in Sagaponack

Louis Begley on *James Biber*

MY WIFE AND I HAD NO PLAN IN 1982 to buy a country house in the Hamptons. In fact, we had told ourselves we would not do any such thing. There were various reasons. The progress of our five children through private schools and universities made our income disappear quicker than it was earned, and ate into our small capital. And we thought we rather liked being summer renters not tied to any particular place, free to move on if our circumstances or mood changed. Until 1978, we had been spending our vacations on Spetsai, a tiny Greek island off the Peloponnesus. New phenomena—daily invasions by hordes of tourists with backpacks and sleeping bags, and price gouging by surly natives—made us uncomfortable. Our thoughts turned to Bridgehampton and Water Mill, where we had friends, and to the gloriously deserted Long Island beaches. We have always made up our minds fast: in the course of one cold April afternoon in '78 we found in Sagaponack a large ramshackle house we liked that could hold our huge family; we rented it on the spot, and returned to it happily summer after summer. Then our landlady installed her son's girlfriend and the girlfriend's baby in the barn on the other side of the garden. We found it impossible to protest. The baby teethed and screamed; the girlfriend yelled at the baby all night and into the telephone all day.

Unwilling to face another season of no sleep, we rented for the summer of '82 a house off Job's Lane in Bridgehampton, which had looked good during a hasty visit but did not withstand closer acquaintance. It was a summer when it seemed to rain every weekend, and most weekdays as well. Unexpectedly, one of our very dear friends, Fernando, a Brazilian who lived in Rio de Janeiro, announced that he was coming to spend a Saturday, Sunday and Monday with us. The prospect filled us with terror: how were we going to keep this elegant and refined young man amused during three sodden days in a house where nothing felt right? As usual, my wife, Anka, came up with the practical solution: let's take him to visit houses for sale, she said, he will like that. Wasting no time, she and our second oldest son, Adam, started looking at real estate ads. In the *New York Times Magazine*, they came upon the photograph of an improbable offering in Sagaponack, north

of Route 27. It seemed to be a one story wooden structure wrapped around a space with a roof of its own made of a peculiar translucent material that did not seem to be glass. Good, we thought, a mystery house! Adam called the number given in the ad and made an appointment for Saturday afternoon. The weekend came, and with it perfect beach weather. We told Adam that he had better tell the architect our plans had changed. You can't do that to him, Adam replied, he is much too nice. We weren't going to argue. Instead, we all got into the car and, after considerable trial and error, at the end of a long driveway snaking through the scrub oak west of Sagg Road, after passing the dwelling pictured in the ad, which turned out to be not for sale, we found the house designed by Jim Biber, now a Pentagram partner.

It was stained gray and consisted of two rectangles of roughly equal length, one lying east-west and the other north-south, joined to make a right triangle without a hypotenuse. The east-west rectangle snuggled against a much taller structure, apparently constructed of the same material as the roof of the other house. We entered the east-west rectangle, since it was nearest to us, through a tiny foyer. Beyond stretched a long living room separated from a small kitchen by a wall that didn't quite reach the ceiling. There was an opening in the wall, for an extension of the kitchen counter, which made me think of the stage of a marionette theater. The north-south rectangle consisted of three fairly small bedrooms, each opening on a long corridor with a gleaming oak floor; the corridor ended at a large master bedroom. A door from that room, which gave the illusion of continuing the corridor, led directly into the woods. There was something about the interior of this house—although it was clearly very practical and somehow matter-of-fact—that struck me as ineffably gay. Was it the profusion of whimsically placed windows of different sizes? The unexpected bow windows in the living room? Or the way in which light poured in through all these apertures? I am still not sure. The fact is

---

Previous spread: Garden courtyard view of the Begley house in Sagaponack, with living room and conservatory (rear) flanked by bedrooms (left) and detached cabin (right).

that all four of us, my wife, Adam, Fernando, and I, were in the best of moods as we listened to the explanation of how this house and the house shown in the ad came to be built in this particular fashion, on speculation. It was a project, we were told, not unlike an architecture school assignment: the task was to design houses that combined the highest standard of modern—some would say postmodern—esthetic with reasonable cost of construction. Two such houses were already in existence and complete; we were standing in the more recent of them. The third would be placed to the north of us. We were to think of them as variations on a theme: wooden rectangles, identical but placed differently, in an architectural conversation with each other and with the structures to which our cicerone somewhat pretentiously, I thought, referred as conservatories. The material used in making the conservatories, which so far as I was concerned, still defied identification, was nothing grander than corrugated plastic, commonly used in the construction of airport hangars. Of course, I said, now I understand. This is a yogurt factory!

In the end, the name conservatory has stuck, but just then I thought that my name fit better that beguiling cube, more than two stories high, with a roof shaped like a pyramid. The corrugated plastic had been bolted onto a scaffolding of beams, which was supported by four very tall steel columns rising from cement pedestals. The floor was made of flagstone. Very quickly we understood the symbiotic relationship between the conservatory and the house: standing in the center of the stone floor one saw the north façade of the house that echoed its south façade on the other side of the living room rectangle. The point of difference was that on the conservatory side there were, in place of bow windows, sliding doors of double pane glass leading indoors. The conservatory, however, had its own multitude of windows and two huge doors, one in the east and one in the west wall. Since the corrugated plastic is not an insulating material—it neither attracts nor repels heat—the conservatory cannot be

Top left: Conservatory interior with gridded wall structure and steel columns. *Left:* Exterior view of conservatory at night, with translucent skin creating the effect of a Japanese lantern.

195

used in cold weather. But when winter comes, it is enough to slide the glass doors shut to find oneself in a warm house that has become smaller and cozier. We were to come to think of the conservatory as our futuristic gazebo, miraculously attached to the house, rather than tucked away in some non-existent part of the garden.

It was Fernando who gave voice to the subversive thought that had perhaps passed through Anka's and my minds as well. You should buy this house, he told us. It's beautiful, and exactly right for you, Adam chimed in, but that wasn't surprising. In our family, if there is an opportunity to spend a large chunk of money, the children root for it. Anka and I, however, lost no time assuring Fernando that this was a bad idea, and gave him the excellent reasons for not investing in real estate I have already cited. And I added one that was very personal: I did not think that I could live in a house that was so modern, so new, and so perfect. The effort of maintaining it in its original condition, of achieving a stasis of perfection, would drive me mad. Nevertheless, I didn't dissent from the plan to return for one more careful look. I particularly wanted to have the next visit take place at the end of the afternoon—during the hour of the mosquito. Mosquitoes are drawn to me irresistibly. I decided to expose myself to them on the west side of the conservatory, in the clearing nearest the woods. If, as I anticipated, they attacked en masse, that would be a sign of the kind that in ancient times seers could read in a flight of birds. It would tell me not to tempt the gods by trying to live face to face with the pristine perfection of this house.

Not a single mosquito disturbed my calm when, two days later, at the stroke of six-thirty in the afternoon, a long gin drink in hand, I began my watch, stoically waiting for the first bite, wondering into what sort of adventure Fernando's chance visit had propelled us. Although I stayed until sunset, I did not hear a single buzz or feel a single sting. The next day, Anka and I toured the house again and said to each other, let's do it. Who knows? Perhaps owning this house will turn out to be good for the whole family. Moving with great speed—as though Anka

understood that I was like a man who has to finish a piece of gooey dessert under the scrutiny of a watchful hostess, and thinks he had better get it over with— we became owners of the house. There were a only a few things we wanted to be done before we moved in, and none of them involved modifying the structure or even the color scheme. We liked the white walls, the pale blue baseboards, and the spinach green metal lamps with an industrial look fixed to the walls like sconces. But we wanted to build a one-room cabin, with a roof that mimicked the conservatory, turning the notional triangle formed by the house into a square. We named it Amey's hut, for our daughter who had asserted the claim to be its first occupant. We also had two smaller huts built with similar roofs, one to the northwest of the conservatory to hold tools, and one by the side of the pool that we had placed far enough from the house to avoid having it in our line of vision. Later the huts became triplets: we added a third to serve as storage space for our Honda scooters and bicycles. We planted flowers, some of them perennials, flowering bushes and trees, and, above all, enough evergreens to make sure that during the winter and the unbearably slow Eastern Long Island spring, when deciduous trees shed their leaves, the eye is drawn to masses of dark green and not to the skeletal and distraught oaks.

In the twenty years of occupancy, we have made only one real structural change. The expansion of our family and of our conception of the comfort and privacy we deserve, led us to dream, a few years ago, of a new and bigger master bedroom. And, of course, a new and better bathroom. Over dinner usually, in restaurants that put a sheet of white paper over the table, Anka and I drew plans for this project, with the guilty feelings of someone about to commit a sacrilege. Whatever we came up with, we were sure, would violate the house and its design. We would be sacrificing beauty and a sense of rightness to comfort; the only thing to do was to give up and stay as we were. Then we asked Jim Biber for help, and told him we thought that our intentions must come to him as a shock. Not at all, he replied, the bedroom rectangle of your house can turn ninety degrees to the east, as though to enclose the lawn and suggest a cloister. That was an idea we had at

Opposite: Entry facade of the Begley house upon completion.

197

the start, he continued, and it was abandoned only because our budget was too small. Once the work has been finished, you won't be able to believe that the house wasn't always like that. Jim was right; the new construction was a change reaffirming the continuity of the original design. It was to rank, like the purchase of the house itself, among our happiest decisions.

And what happened, a reader might ask, to my fear of living in a modern house? I am tempted to answer that the house and I have matured together. At first, infatuated with its good looks, the clarity of its lines and finish, and the way it exposed itself so bravely to light, I did struggle to maintain the illusion of its virginity. My efforts were various, and productive of great amusement for the whole family. During the hours when I should have been at my desk, I could regularly be observed wandering through the house, a bottle of Fantastic in one hand, a wad of paper towel in the other, in search of finger marks and traces of other indignities, many of which were visible only to me, that I could wash off walls and doors. Sometimes these efforts turned out to be inadequate, and I repainted a section of the wall. Afterward, for days on end I would inspect my work and worry whether the new paint took the light differently from the old, whether it wasn't more offensive than the stain I had tried to remove. My cares extended, of course, to the outdoors as well, particularly the condition of the patio on the west side of the conservatory and the flagstones we had put down on the path leading to the swimming pool. There, my special enemy was gravel; I found its incursions on the surface of the stones to be a personal affront calling for swift retribution. I would start sweeping. The spectacle I offered, repeated any number of times a day unless it was raining, delighted the children. On my birthday they gave me ceremoniously a fine straw broom with a red handle. The card declared that this was my Stradivarius.

I would explain to one and all, in defense of my compulsive cleaning, that it was the inevitable result of

*Left: Detail of the Begley house's conservatory walls, punctured by windows and doors that allow the space to be transformed into an oversize porch. **Opposite:** Recent addition of a bedroom and bathroom built on the garden courtyard.*

a mismatch. I was meant to live in an old, preferably Victorian, dark-paneled house, with secret, rarely ventured into passages, where sunlight fills only spaces that have to be scrubbed every day: the kitchen and the bathrooms. The toll that time and careless hands took on such a dwelling would pass unseen, sparing me constant torment. Such bravura passages duly entered our family folklore. In the meantime, eyes wide open, I soaked up the charm of our young and vulnerable house, in all seasons and in every kind of weather, finding that when we were in it, not even diluvial rainstorms and lowering skies could make us feel gloomy. Too much light had been hoarded inside it. And I was grateful for its capacity to expand into a large family house in the spring, summer and early fall, when we use the conservatory as our principal living space, and the idea of giving a lunch or dinner for twenty-four doesn't faze us at all, and then to contract and withdraw into itself once we close the conservatory, so that, when Anka and I are in Sagaponack alone for an occasional winter weekend or for the Christmas vacation, our house seems to have been conceived from the start for a couple of rather contented empty-nesters. Empty-nesters living inside a Japanese paper lantern. That is how the house looks and feels when the windows are ablaze, and the conservatory becomes a yellow cube glowing against the night sky.

With love comes tolerance for change. The wrinkles on the face of a woman with whom we live happily, that were the object of our dread when we were young, because we thought that their advent would cause us unbearable pain, in fact make her face dearer, and perhaps more beautiful, because they bear witness to the victories and defeats of a shared existence. One must not confuse houses or animals or plants with people. But houses too are our companions on a long and difficult journey, and we can read in them the log of our adventures. So I still wipe off errant stains, and occasionally I wield my broom at the most inopportune moments. But I do so without anguish, in the knowledge that so far our house and we have aged well, with decent grace.

Left: Freestanding bedroom cabin, built to accommodate the Begleys' extended family.

A Texas Daredevil

Robert Draper on *DJ Stout*

GUY WALKS INTO A BAR, SITS DOWN, orders a margarita. Three drinks later, he slides discreetly off of his bar stool. Like a heat-seeking missile, he homes in on a clutter of denim-clad and elaborately lipsticked patrons. Standing over the gaggle, he offers what is surely the most memorable line they are likely to hear that evening and in the evenings to follow during this summer of 1992: "Would you buy an issue of *Texas Monthly* if it had H. Ross Perot on the cover?"

And they stare back up at him, this brown-eyed and grizzle-cheeked stranger, who until he opened his mouth seemed as close to George Clooney as anyone in this remote West Texas town is likely to get. Their own eyes darken with alarm. Then one of them giggles. The others laugh as well. The stranger offers an asymmetrical grin. Okay, they're thinking with palpable relief—so the guy has a sense of humor. Perot on the cover. Good one. You may be seated. You may proceed to buy the next seven rounds.

Except that he's not kidding. "I mean, a funny image," he persists, "with a headline that says"—and here he expels some perhaps not immortal blurb in a bedazzled stage whisper. Now their unease returns. Where is this going?

Where it's going is that (as he informs the young women) his name is DJ Stout, he's the art director for *Texas Monthly,* and he's thinking about cover images. And faster than a dust storm, he's all over them. Perot as the quintessence of Texas bluster. Perot as topic A of the national political consciousness. This image, that subhead, sketches on margarita-soaked napkins… and if they were not exactly rapt at the beginning of this inquisition, it is by now clear to them that the stranger does not intend to leave so easily, and anyway, he *is* rather cute in a lopsided kind of way and, he *did* buy, well, *a* round. And anyway, they figure, Prince Charming must be on the next stagecoach. Until then, the art director and his cover images will have to do.

I hope it doesn't spoil the tableau to record that I was there that evening and that the art director stuck me with the tab. In fact, the performance was well worth it, if only to confirm the depths of DJ Stout's obsessions and the lengths to which he will go

Opposite: Texas Monthly, *design and art direction, 1987–2000.*

202

An Insider's Guide to Texas Amusement Parks ★ Beat the Lottery!

Texas Monthly

JUNE 1992 · $2.50

WHAT,
ME
PRESIDENT?

HOW PEROT CAN WIN
by Paul Burka

HOW PEROT
PLAYS HARDBALL
A Partner's Story

ROSS
92

0 37405   06   735995

METROPOLIS

GEHRY • HERZOG & DE MEURON

ARCHITECTURE < CULTURE > DESIGN

October 2003

ARCHITECTS

An alarming new
analysis of global
warming says
architects are the
problem—and
our best solution.

POLLUTE

to seize upon an idea and then hawk it as if it were God's own pocketknife. He was relentless that night, fevered with self-certainty and utterly shameless. By the end of it all, I believe he sold a few advance copies. And I got to hear the same pitch, albeit a more sober version, two days later, at an editorial meeting at *Texas Monthly*—one of countless exhibitions of DJ Stout's ferocious vaudevilles I had the pleasure to witness.

One afternoon, a few years after we had both left the magazine, I visited his office to discuss a book project in which we had both been enlisted. I found DJ hovering over a drafting table, wearing his familiar do-not-approach-man-at-work glower. Hearing my footsteps, DJ looked up, grinned, and threw me something. It was a Campbell's soup can. Or rather, it was an invitation to an art opening affixed to a soup can. A Warhol-esque gambit, of course, but DJ Stout has always been a ruthless scavenger, long before sampling and appropriation entered the annals of acceptable practice. More to the point: For weeks thereafter, if you were an Austinite and didn't have a canned invitation sitting on your coffee table, you might as well have been exiled to Tora Bora.

For those uncertain about what it means to be a Texan, I give you DJ Stout. Though to the untrained eye he may project a coastal suaveness, this object of international repute in the world of design media bears all the telltale traits of a landlocked Lone Star lifer. He is powerfully self-reliant, fueled by a bottomless reservoir of faith not only in himself but in all human possibility—a true disciple, in other words, of the Texas Myth that to achieve immortality, one must only be bold enough to reach for it. His exuberance and his daredevilry and his reflexive big-think are the stuff of yesteryear's oil wildcatters. You might remember, of course, that such entrepreneurs harbored a ruthless streak. Not that I ever saw a violent side to DJ, but no one else at the magazine where we worked together for seven years exhibited his capacity for in-house junkyard-dog brawling. He politicked, he wheedled, he threatened, he persisted, he flattered, he hollered. God, was he a pain in the ass! But when it came to getting a magazine-cover

Opposite: Metropolis, *magazine cover design, 2003.*
Right: Guitar Player, *magazine redesign, 2004.*

idea ratified, DJ Stout had more notches on his belt than the rest of us combined.

Texas sprawls along the psychic fault line separating progressivism and traditionalism, between worshipfulness and blasphemy. DJ has mined that no-man's-land to spectacular effect. He superimposed Governor Ann Richards's famous visage onto that of a Harley motorcycle rider, which infuriated Richards until people began asking her to autograph their issue of *Texas Monthly* with the "White Hot Mama" cover image. He morphed 1992 presidential candidate Perot's face into that of *Mad Magazine*'s Alfred E. Neuman. He caught Anna Nicole Smith winking during a photo shoot and thereby cast her as a lurid Lone Star version of Marilyn Monroe. Like any Texas high roller, DJ didn't always walk out of the

casino with his pockets bulging. Once he commissioned Mary Ellen Mark to tour the state and photograph rodeo participants. The prints Mark brought back utterly defied the phony pageantry to which Texans have long subscribed. Certain staffers were appalled by the grim expressions. (I loved them.) DJ ran one such image on the cover. That issue bombed. Nonetheless, the gamble was memorable: By prodding an icon, he prodded our imagination.

That said, there exists no more fervent iconist in the media-design world than DJ Stout. Being from the southern nub of West Texas (read: cowboys, Indians, cattle barons, oilmen, banditos, drug lords), his fascination with the skywalkers and the archvillains is neither contrived nor patronizing. That authenticity of reverence and reference showed in the magnificent send-up of the Texas Rangers law enforcement legends that DJ commissioned in 1994—probably *Texas Monthly*'s most successful photo spread ever. The Rangers were shot in dignified, timeless black and white, a Stout staple (not

Below left: The American Quarter Horse Racing Journal. *Below right:* America's Horse. *Opposite (left and right):* The American Quarter Horse Journal. *All three official publications of the American Quarter Horse Association redesigned in 2001.*

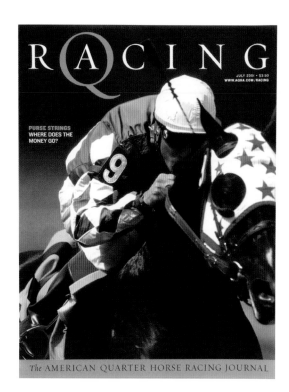

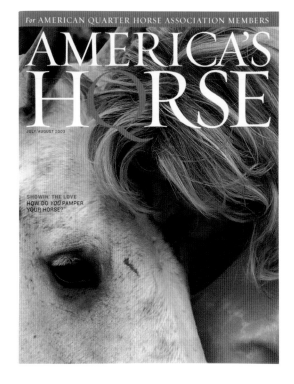

to mention vintage Pentagram). Six years later, he would design *Outside* magazine's first black-and-white cover. That image was of cyclist-for-the-ages Lance Armstrong, knotty arms folded about his chest. Straightforward, unmistakable, a commercial bonanza. And when given the trickier assignment of consulting with the American Bar Association's trade publication on a paltry budget, DJ eschewed the usual dreary insider photos and yawner headlines. Instead, he brought in famous illustrators like Brad Holland to convey, in a simple black-and-white sketch, the kind of heroic symbolism that few high-dollar photo studios can hope to replicate.

There are two areas in which DJ Stout deviates from the stereotype incubated in his native state. First, he is not gaudy. Though as a designer he belongs to no faith except the Church of Whatever Works, his preferences run to the clean and the classical. While most magazine covers are splattered with punchy teases (More Orgasms! J-Lo Talks Dirty!), the Stout-era *Texas Monthly* purveyed cover

messages that registered like a kiss rather than an assault. Such nuance lends itself to lasting works. Though he achieved fame as one of America's pre-eminent magazine art directors, I frankly think DJ's best work lies in book design. Under his directorship, modest novels gleam like fine minerals, photo collections are thematically precise, and a barbecue-recipe collection is freighted with the authority of a hallowed text. Even a somber recapitulation of a black man's infamous dragging death in Jasper, Texas, is dealt with so gently that the ghastly subject matter becomes approachable in the process.

The second non-Texan trait he exhibits is a bizarre absence of ego. I don't want to be misinterpreted here: No one who wears black in the Austin summer and changes hairstyles with every paycheck as DJ Stout does could be accused of abject modesty. Still, he never chased his vanity all the way to New York, even though by the mid-'90s virtually every magazine in America was bidding for his services. Plainly put, DJ stuck it out with *Texas Monthly*

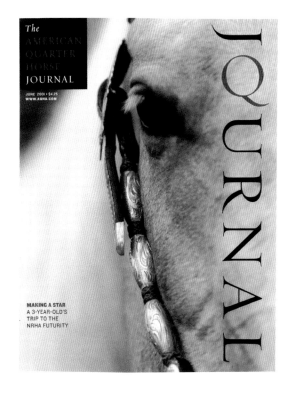

because that's where he thought he could do the best work. His art budget was small, but the power he wielded was not; and with all those pages and a rash of wild notions at his disposal, he lured the nation's finest photographers to his Texas fiefdom.

Leibovitz. Wegman. Seliger. Mark. Newton. Kern. Avedon. DJ appealed to their self-esteem, their curiosity, whatever it took. (One thing it took was respect. DJ always understood the full constitution of photographic art. If he couldn't offer big bucks, he could assure the visiting masters that their work would be painstakingly reproduced and laid out as if on fine gallery walls.) Appalachian documentarist Shelby Lee Adams was enchanted to discover a kindred feeling in the woods of East Texas. Leibovitz protégé Max Aguilera-Hellweg sought to trace his ancestry along the Mexican border. James Evans became a

statewide star in DJ's pages, Keith Carter a national one, Dan Winters—well. I remember DJ showing me some spread Dan had done for *Outside* in the summer of 1991 and telling me, "This guy's gonna get hot. I want him now." And of course DJ got him, and though there is no way to prove conclusively that the dozen or so collaborations over the next few years catapulted Winters to a fame that perhaps already awaited him, I can tell you this: It was under DJ Stout's directorship that Dan Winters went from damned good to great. And as far as anyone could tell, it didn't bother DJ Stout in the least that his photographers got the fame. After all, he got the images.

I tried not to laugh when I heard that Lands' End intended to use DJ Stout to redesign a couple of its catalog covers. That's like bringing in General Patton to oversee a boot-camp mess hall.

He did the covers just fine, of course. Before long, he was reconfiguring the actual content, installing narratives into otherwise bland and static pages. But then DJ brought up a more encompassing issue:

Opposite and below: Brand identity for Lands' End, a direct merchant of products for the home and traditionally styled apparel.

Why did the men's, children's, and home catalogs each feature a different logo? Shouldn't the moniker be recognizable? Shouldn't it suggest the Lands' End brand? Wasn't there equity to be traded on here? And so DJ was commissioned to codify the logo—a fox-in-the-henhouse scenario if there ever was one, with the end result that the logo itself was redesigned. Out with the flaccid, ambiguous typeface; in with a clean, distinctive look immediately transferable to any number of merchandising schemes.

But DJ Stout was merely gaining locomotion. One day he approached Lands' End's creative director, Lee Eisenberg, who had once been the editor of *Esquire* magazine and had attempted to hire DJ back in the '90s. Why, he asked, didn't the company have a symbol? Like Nike's swoosh or Polo's

pony? DJ was treading on thin ice here. Lands' End is not headquartered in New York City, or even in Austin—but rather, in Dodgeville, Wisconsin, where midwestern sturdiness predominates and change is a four-letter word. He anticipated this, of course. In their research he and his Pentagram cohorts had uncovered, somewhere in the dusky annals of company lore, the use of a striped lighthouse in an early logo. So no, he insisted to Eisenberg, what he had in mind wasn't at all a deviation from company tradition—but rather an embrace of it.

So now we have navy blue caps with the striped etchings of a lighthouse emblazoned in full view. And Lands' End becomes more than the sum total of its inventory. Tomorrow the world. Pilfering from the past to anoint the future. I haven't seen DJ Stout in a year or so, but I doubt he's changed much. I doubt sincerely that he's at rest. Somewhere in a bar on any given night, there's a cocktail napkin with his latest vision on it. I'd save the napkin if I were at that table. Granted, restlessness comes cheap at such places. Restless talent does not.

Opposite: The History of Japanese Photography, *book design, published by Yale University Press in association with the Museum of Fine Arts, Houston, 2003.* ***Below:*** Ezekiel's Horse, *photographs by Keith Carter, published by the University of Texas Press in association with the Wittliff Gallery Series, 2000.*

Building Language

Paul Goldberger on *Michael Gericke*

I AM SUPPOSED TO BE WRITING about Michael Gericke, not about his work, since this book is a collection of essays on people, not a set of statements about design. The problem is that I can't separate out Michael Gericke from his work. I haven't seen him with his family, or working on his house in Brooklyn, or spending time in his hometown in Wisconsin, or doing whatever else he does when work is far from his mind. I am not sure, actually, whether work is ever far from Michael Gericke's mind, which is to say not that he is obsessive but rather that he is one of those people lucky enough to spend his career satisfying his own curiosity. He grew up as the son of a banker in the rural Midwest and showed no interest either in banking or in staying there. He started out thinking he wanted to be a ceramicist and went on to the University of Wisconsin to study fine arts.

"I thought I would throw pots my whole life," Gericke said to me, but that was when he was sitting in a conference room at Pentagram in New York, by which time it had long become clear how far he had come both from Wisconsin and from Boulder, Colorado, where Gericke began his career as a designer at Communication Arts, a partnership founded by two veterans of the Charles and Ray Eames office. He took his first job, he said, because "I wanted to ski out west." He stayed in Boulder for seven years, did relatively little skiing, but was exposed to a multidisciplinary approach to design. In 1984, he went to New Orleans as a member of the design team for the World's Fair, the exposition whose theme structure was a strange and fanciful creation by Charles Moore called the Wonderwall.

It is possible to think of Gericke's life as a series of casual accidents, and he seems to enjoy giving that impression. The pivotal moment in his university education—the moment when he began to think of the potential of graphic design—was when he encountered a professor who had led the United Airlines design program and hired Saul Bass to develop its identity. Seeing the United program, Gericke said, was when he "saw how to reach and affect a much broader audience," something he came to understand that he actually cared quite a bit about.

Opposite: Identity for the Center for Architecture, New York, 2001.

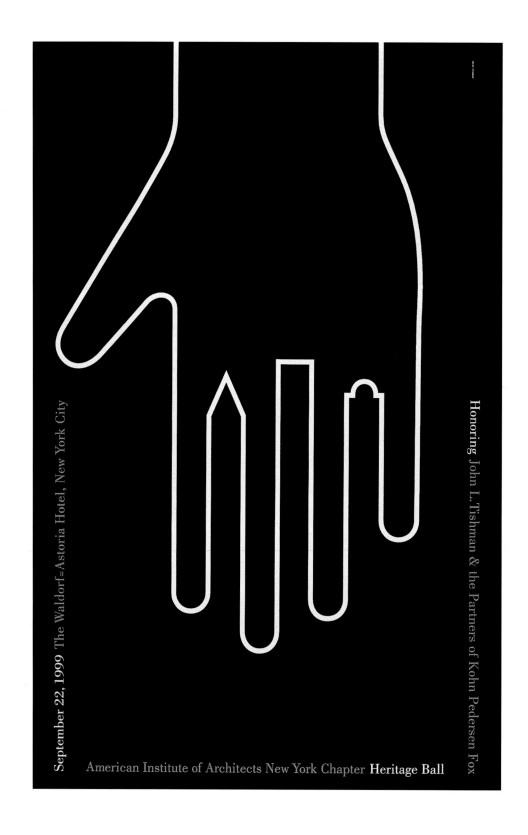

September 22, 1999 The Waldorf=Astoria Hotel, New York City

Honoring John L. Tishman & the Partners of Kohn Pedersen Fox

American Institute of Architects New York Chapter **Heritage Ball**

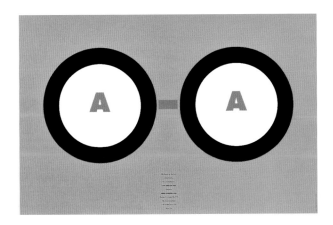

Gericke is affable, and his easygoing nature allows him, like many midwesterners, to appear far less ambitious than he is. It is not possible for someone this friendly to be driven, you think, since he is not in the slightest obsequious, and his warmth is perfectly punctuated by reserve. He is enthusiastic, but he does not force his enthusiasms on others. He listens, and he is genuinely curious about the way things work, and you realize after you have been talking to him for a while that he has teased out of you more observations and information than you have got from him. If he were not a good graphic designer, he might have been a decent therapist. Then again, good designers are always, in part, good therapists. Gericke is soft on the surface and sharp underneath, and he sees more than he lets on, and he lets his clients do the talking, at least for a while.

He has built a practice at Pentagram with many facets but with a unique relation to architecture—both graphics within architecture that lead people through complicated places, like airports ("wayfinding," in current parlance), and graphics about architecture, such as the remarkable series of posters and printed materials he has created to shape a new identity for the New York chapter of the American Institute of Architects (AIA). Gericke didn't seek this kind of work at first. He didn't even have a particular interest in architecture. "I wasn't an avid follower of architecture—I couldn't name a dozen architects in the city when I first came to New York," he told me. His first work at Pentagram (where he began in 1985, and in 1993 became one of the first partners ever to rise from the ranks) consisted largely of corporate-identity assignments.

In 1995 the AIA called Gericke and asked for help. The AIA was increasingly becoming known as an organization that cared more about architects' pay scales than about the quality of design, and they were particularly concerned about the image of the group in New York, which is theoretically the nation's capital of design. They told Gericke he needed to make the local chapter of the AIA appear to be "much more driven by design, not professional

*Left: Poster for the American Institute of Architects 1995 Heritage Ball honoring architect Philip Johnson. **Opposite:** Poster for the American Institute of Architects 1999 Heritage Ball.*

practice issues." It was a particular challenge, since he not only needed to give the AIA an identity that would appear unusually sophisticated; he had to shape its image in such a way as to be approachable to the organization's broad range of members, many of whom would have been somewhat suspicious of an instant remake into the avant-garde. And he had to give the AIA materials a clearly architectural slant—they had to feel as if they belonged to this organization and only this organization. In some way that was not too obvious, the images had to be about buildings, or about architects.

Gericke started with what he saw. In one of his first posters, designed for the Heritage Ball honoring Philip Johnson, he used Johnson's famous heavy round black eyeglass frames as the iconic image, against a bright yellow background, with an *A* inside each circle and a small *I* in between, turned on its side. The poster was bold, simple, direct, and memorable. So, too, with Gericke's poster for the same event two years later, honoring I.M. Pei: two of Pei's pyramids at the Louvre, against a red background, with a bold *I* in between. For another event, held at Windows on the World at the World Trade Center, Gericke shaped the twin towers into a pair of straight, slender *A*'s, with a ghostly hint of an *I* in between, eerily foreshadowing the "towers of light" memorial that would be created years later after the towers were destroyed.

In each case, Gericke was not so much inventing a form as using what was there in a way that no one else had thought of doing: abstracting a set of architectural forms into powerful graphic images. In the AIA work he managed to create a sense of freshness and energy at no cost to dignity; the pieces, including the remarkable covers he did for the AIA journal *Oculus*, are eye grabbing and crisp, and yet they invariably have a certain formality and poise.

Gericke is a master not only of composition but of tone. You could feel that particularly in a pair of much later projects that brought him back to the World Trade Center after September 11—the identity and graphic materials for New York New Visions, the consortium of design professionals whose work ultimately had a significant effect on the design parameters for the rebuilding of Lower Manhattan, and the graphic design for the viewing wall that now surrounds the Ground Zero site itself.

The New York New Visions graphics were more factual than the AIA work and far less exuberant; to do otherwise would have been interpreted as insufficiently respectful of the seriousness of the moment, but Gericke was able to give the graphics a sense of both elegance and gravitas, and he struck the balance perfectly. As with the AIA, his clients were designers, but unlike the AIA, his audience was not. It was a two-pronged challenge. On the one hand, while the architects, planners, and graphic and industrial designers of New York New Visions shared a common cause, they didn't share a common identity. On the other hand, the materials they were producing—their own responses to the events of September 11—had to speak to an even more diverse audience of besieged politicians and government officials. Gericke's efforts gave a dignified presence and conceptual clarity to the group's public information materials—securing both the attention of beleaguered decision makers and the credibility of the consortium. New York New Visions emerged as a leader in widening the search for an appropriate response to the tragedy. Their ambitious plans and aspirations were given distinction at the same time they were made transparent.

So, too, with the complicated series of information panels and tributes, developed with Robert Davidson of the Port Authority of New York and New Jersey, that are an integral part of the viewing wall at the former World Trade Center site. They are not too stylish, which would somehow have seemed to trivialize the horrific events of September 11, yet nor are they too casual, which would have robbed the panels of the dignity that they require. Against a simple gridded transparent wall that allows unobstructed views for all visitors to Ground Zero, Gericke combined black-and-white photographs and historical text depicting the rich history of Lower Manhattan and the rise and fall of the twin towers. In moving from public advocacy to public event, indeed, to the site itself, Gericke's design process was even more inclusive—taking into account the needs of the Port Authority; the concerns of the victims'

Opposite: Wayfinding program for the new Terminal One at Lester B. Pearson International Airport, Toronto, 2003.

BUILDING THE EMPIRE STATE BLASTING ALL CONSTRUCTION RECORDS & RISING
A STORY A DAY TO BECOME, FOR FORTY YEARS, THE WORLD'S TALLEST BUILDING
EXHIBITION OPENS OCTOBER 1998, 16 WALL STREET THE SKYSCRAPER MUSEUM

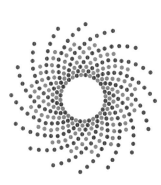

BROOKLYN
HISTORICAL
SOCIETY

families, downtown business owners, and residents; and the myriad politics of rebuilding. While the wall does, in fact, list the names of all the victims, it has never been considered a memorial. It is simply a place where anyone can observe the work under way at Ground Zero and remember.

It is in the wayfinding work that Gericke seems increasingly at home, in effect collaborating with architects and planners to give their buildings an identity and make them read coherently to their users. He especially enjoys his role as part of a larger team. He sees his work as "making the machinery of the building function," but he knows it is much more than that, especially since he is only really comfortable dealing with buildings and architects whose work would interest him. For the new Toronto international airport terminal, a sleek structure designed by Skidmore, Owings & Merrill with Moshe Safdie, Gericke was presented with a good piece of architecture but a triple problem—the annoyingly inflexible aspects of any airport layout, which are enough to frustrate most users, however appealing the graphics may be; the Canadian requirement that all signs be in two languages; and the soaring, glass-enclosed terminal whose visual drama could overshadow any graphics. Collaborating with Entro Communications in Toronto, Gericke arrived at a solution in the form of signs that used exceptionally clear and logical icons, color coding by user path, and shape to make distinctions. English is placed on convex surfaces, and French on flat ones, and by giving all of the major signs both flat and curving sections, Gericke ended up with a shape that subtly and gently echoes the section of the main terminal building itself.

For Safdie's Salt Lake City Public Library, Gericke and his team devised a simple iconic image, a square with a series of vertical lines of various thicknesses, some at slight angles, an abstraction of a shelf of books. This icon, and a simple informational typeface, was used in several contexts throughout the building to unify the graphic

Top left: Identity for the Skyscraper Museum, New York, 1997. Left: Identity for the Brooklyn Historical Society, 2003. Opposite: Poster for an exhibition on the building of the Empire State Building at the Skyscraper Museum, New York, 1998.

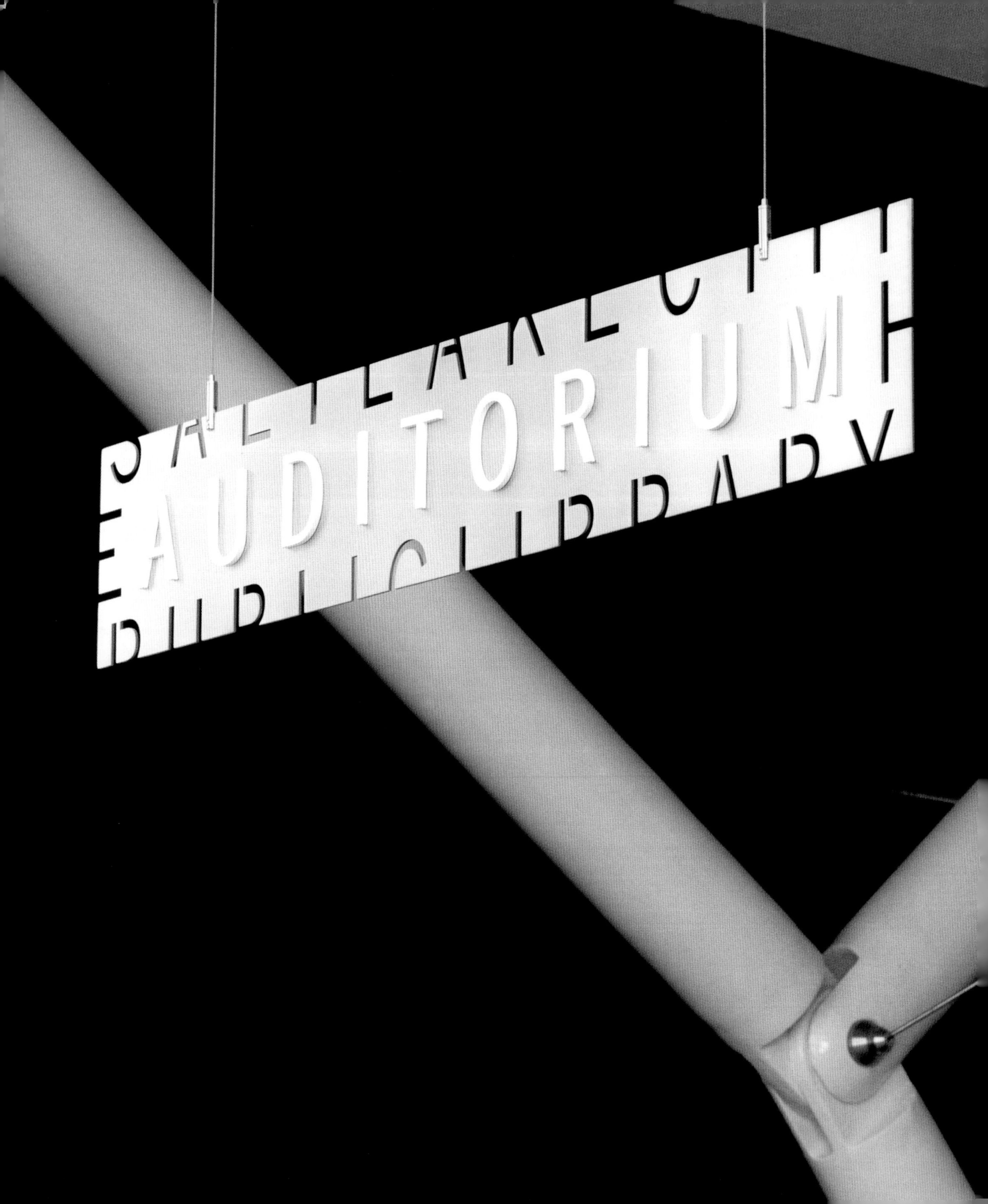
AUDITORIUM

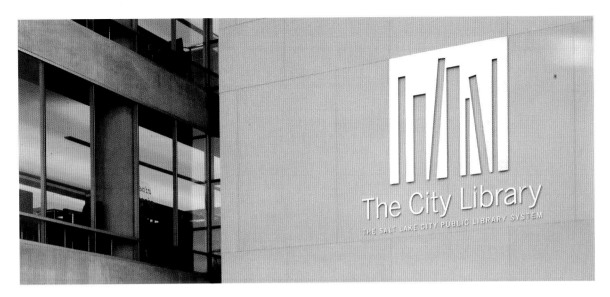

program. But—and this is where it is uniquely Gericke's, I think—it also sends the viewer critical and subtle messages about the building itself. The lines are clean and modern, as the architecture is, but the arrangement of books is casual and informal, with books leaning on each other as they might on a shelf at home. It is a perfect way to send the message that the library is inviting and its attitude toward books is relaxed, not institutional. Gericke's informational graphics in stainless steel indicating various departments, on the other hand, have only type, but here he has placed the name of the department—Young Adults, Fiction, Film—in letters across the middle of the panel, with the name of the library sliced off and surrounding the signs. The partial characters read almost as abstractions or as a kind of decorative ornament around the main message, but they also serve to tie the various messages together. Gericke describes these signs, also developed with Entro, as "similar to the experience of reading, when you continually discover words within the context of other words"; there is a kind of celebration of type and letters here, and while that is something graphic designers do all the time, it is rare that they are able to do it in such harmony with the architecture.

Opposite: Wayfinding graphics for the Salt Lake City Public Library, 2003. **Above:** *Identity for the Salt Lake City Public Library System, 2003.*

You sense when you look at these signs that Gericke is caressing the words, which is very much like a graphic designer, but that he is also caressing the material and the texture and the scale and the mass, which is very much like an architect. He is not afraid of image, and he is not one of those designers who think only in terms of fonts and the proportion of white space to type. He likes pictures, and he likes things that emerge out of the reality of specific situations, like the exhilarating poster he did for the Skyscraper Museum's exhibition on the Empire State Building, which showed the Empire State literally blasting off like a rocket. (Nearly as enticing is his logo for the museum, which by turning the profile of the Empire State into a gigantic *S* creates the most inventive acknowledgment of its status as the platonic skyscraper that I have ever seen.)

What ties Gericke's images together, beyond their inherent formal elegance, is a sense that he comes to every problem fresh and searches to find the essential qualities of the object he is representing. It is that quest which comes before any forms he brings to the table, and while he has his stylistic preferences, he does not begin with them. He manages to get them in there somehow—I didn't see much in the way of ornate type or clutter or fussiness—but every design he does so closely connects to something about its subject that you feel as if the designer had merely coaxed forth its true nature, and presented it with grace.

Anti-Manner

Rose George on *Fernando Gutiérrez*

ON ANY GIVEN EVENING, if things are convivial, Fernando Gutiérrez might get out his tricks—a matchbox that rises up and down, a Coke can that fills on its own. His favorite act, though, is one he calls levitation: Standing at a certain angle, with a certain number of onlookers, he can lift one leg, and the other seems to float.

These tricks aren't spectacular. They can be had for a few pounds at most, in any magic shop. But there's a reason Fernando loves them: In the tricks, there is illusion. Behind the illusion, there is craft. And anchoring the craft there is belief, or soul, or heart, or however you describe the indefinable spirit that turns something good into something better.

These are the qualities you get, if you get Fernando. Take a copy of *Matador*, the luscious and dramatic annual magazine published in Madrid. Drink from a bottle of Telmo Rodriguez's wine, whose labels are Fernando's. Carry a transparent gift-shop bag from the Prado, Spain's national museum, where Fernando has been creative director since January 2003. These objects are different, but together. In their clean, pure lines, their sustained restraint. But most of all, in their appropriateness, no matter who the client. "With Fernando," says the Prado's director, Miguel Zugaza, "design is not just a solution. It's an evaluation."

I learned this in 2000, at *Colors* magazine, where I had previously worked for three years, where Fernando had art-directed Tibor Kalman's no-words issue in 1995 and where he returned that year as creative director. Fernando had already taken the magazine—brash, inventive, but tired—and turned it on its head, with a cool yet emotional issue about a Tanzanian refugee camp. The cutouts, the white backgrounds, the in-your-face magazine of Tibor Kalman were all "stripped down to the bare minimum." The result was older, perhaps, less flashy. Quieter. Proving you don't have to yell to be heard.

I'd returned to write the second issue of "new" *Colors*, on a town called Trash, a Roma settlement in Macedonia. So Fernando and I both found ourselves in the gray concrete of the *Colors* offices at Benetton's "creative center" Fabrica, a Tadao Ando-designed bunker at the end of a bus line in the

Opposite: Matador *magazine (issue G), 2003.*

222

MATADOR

Venetian countryside. And we were arguing. The cover was to be a Roma boy, standing with attitude before a starry photo-studio backdrop. He looked great, but he was dressed head to toe in Nike. It looked like an ad, said Fernando, and he erased the swooshes. I thought differently: that the kid had chosen his clothing with care, for the Saturday-night strutting fest, that there was a good reason for it.

Fernando said nothing, and I took it as an argument lost. Two months later, the issue appeared, Nike intact. I had learned what all Fernando's clients say about him: He listens, though he might not seem to. He will make decisions on criteria that are simple and inviolable: Behind everything, there must be good faith, honesty. What he calls "intention." The swooshes might be the design equivalent of nails scraping a blackboard, but if they mean something, they get to stay.

His silence back then wouldn't surprise me today. This isn't a man who likes talking about himself, because he'd rather get back to work. Why discuss past projects when there are things to be done? Maybe this is why he likes editorial design, why he wanted to design a newspaper supplement, the groundbreaking *Tentaciones*, for Spanish newspaper *El País*: because it's fast, transient. Or maybe not. "Careful," he says, when I pick up an issue of *Matador*, which he also art-directs. "Those are collector's items." *Tentaciones* made his name and that of Grafica, the Barcelona-based studio he co-founded in 1993. But it is magazines he loves. Things that stay alive, that you wouldn't consider discarding, because they're like nothing else. Things like *Matador* and *Colors*, that are bemusing. "I like the

Above: Tentaciones, *a weekly supplement to Spanish newspaper* El País, *1994.* **Opposite:** Tentaciones *redesigned, 2001.*

fact that kiosks don't know where to put them. Though that might mean they're really successful, or a total failure."

Fernando's editorial work didn't really start till he moved to Spain, after seven years with Mike Dempsey at CDT Design. Perhaps it was an inevitable move for a kid from Paddington with Spanish parents, who spent his days at an English school and his evenings at a Spanish one, and whose holidays were with farming relatives in Asturias. But take care with cliché, which dictates that a child of two cultures must personify two national stereotypes. Which pairs a cool English exterior and a Latin passion within. Ice and fire, rigor and passion. It's a truth, but not the whole one.

"I do burn up inside," says Fernando, Hispanically. When he sees something beautiful—an Eduardo Chillida sculpture, Titian's portrait of the pope— when something he is working on is going right. And

then the Londoner returns. "But that's so cheesy. You can't write that."

If we must talk of Spanishness and Englishness, he thinks, then it's not about passion, which is everywhere. It's a way of seeing things that has been shaped by place and time. "The Spanish are fascinated with going forward, because they want to run away from the past. They have a willingness to embrace the future with no qualms." History becomes a reference in the rearview mirror, not a weight. But it pays to keep an eye on it. As the Prado's Zugaza says, "He takes the the past but makes his contribution." Classically modern, and the other way round, too.

Tentaciones had been going a while when a Spanish newspaper's managing editor decided to do something different. The result was the sumptuous, lavish *Matador*, its weight and gravity the opposite of a newspaper, like its ambition. Each issue of

Matador will take one of the twenty-nine letters of the Spanish alphabet. It will finish in 2022, when Fernando is sixty. And this, to him, is a delight, and a risk. Same as running Maupassant's *Le Horla*, in its entirety, on a pistachio background. "If it's well written, you see the pictures in your head."

Ask Fernando to explain how he designs editorial pages, and he will look nonplussed. "I just do." Ask about inspiration, and he will say he gets it "from everything." But then he will say something about codes, harmony, balance. He lays down a path, he says, that others can follow. But where are these codes, I ask? "In my head." Push a bit more, and he says it's about being "into it. Being into the inside of a picture, what's going behind it, what's next to it, is that typeface kerned with a track 2 or at 0…" and he trails off. "A lot of that is boring. But craft is what makes you different to the rest. It's time-consuming and it's invisible."

Even so, the man who believes bus tickets should be beautiful can still love a masterpiece of amateurishness like *Found* magazine, published in Chicago by Davy Rothbart and filled with found notes, pictures, and curses left on car windshields, because design "isn't about eight inks and three varnishes." He can rave about a picture of a tiny toe bone, 780,000 years old, that fills the cover of the *Matador* "Iberian/Ibérico" issue, though the photo isn't great, the lighting off-key. The strength comes from the idea.

This isn't to say the props are unimportant: The covers of the Argentinean publisher Losada, which recruited Fernando in September 2002, are, he points out with pleasure, three different direct Pantone inks. So it's flatter and more intense. Untrained eyes might not pick it up, but they'll notice something different. Something "raw, but pure." For the logo, he redrew Losada's original logo from the early twentieth century, so that it suited a publisher whose catalog swings between past (fifty percent of its titles are classics) and future (the rest is new writing).

Making sense makes more sense than gizmo-led design. Fernando loves drawing, but any pen will do.

Left: Identity for Compañía de Vinos Telmo Rodríguez, 2002. **Opposite:** *Wine bottles for Compañía de Vinos Telmo Rodríguez; (from left to right) LZ, Altos de Lanzaga, and Lanzaga, 2001–02.*

His laptop would be considered ancient by most of Soho. Maybe it's not surprising to anyone who has seen the *Matador* issue F, whose theme is fear, where the typeface is classic IBM Courier, because "it's like computers taking over, like in Kubrick's *2001: A Space Odyssey*." Whatever the reason, the result is design from the inside out, not the other way round. "If you cut him off from humankind for the next forty years," says Leslie Mello, a former colleague, "he'd still be making beautiful things when we saw him in 2043. He can be innovative and very clever within his design, but he's not trying to reinvent it." Nor does he want to stamp it. "All I want to do is stay behind things."

Hence the geographical elusiveness. When he was based in Barcelona, people thought he lived in Madrid. His Madrid friends weren't sure where he lived. Now that he's in London, he spends half his time in Spain. It's one way to keep a distance.

Through *Matador*, Fernando met Telmo Rodríguez, an innovative young winemaker. A child of seven generations of winemaking in Rioja, Rodríguez took old vineyards and revitalized the wines, then sold them only for export. For four years he had been looking for someone to design labels for him. No one, it seemed, understood what he wanted: to create a new identity that reflected the new Spain, not the old one hampered by civil war, recrimination, and regret. Someone who understood how to be local and global, like he was, who appreciated his efforts to give Spanish wine a new, dynamic taste. Fernando and Telmo met and talked, then Telmo got nervous. "I thought—this is a really good designer, and what if I don't like it?" The first bottle arrived. It was the Dehesa Gago Toro with a *g* screen-printed onto glass, its serif a bull's horn, to reflect the Toro region it was made in. Nicely balanced between originality and respect. It fit.

Telmo likes the fact that Fernando's wine knowledge isn't vast. But yet, Fernando gets it. On the wall at the Rodríguez house is a steel contraption that Fernando thought was a sculpture. He suggested using it for the label for Pegaso. Telmo was dumbfounded: the steel structure was an old spring mattress that had served for decades as the gate for the Pegaso vineyard. It was serendipitous, though it still needed work. "At first on the label, the mattress was at the top, and the brand name at the bottom, but Fernando wanted to change it. I didn't agree, but he was right." With the mattress in its right place, it created a line of mountains, with the springs becoming mountainside vineyards. It was "a funny idea that became outstanding." He loves Fernando's labels "because they don't look like they've been done by a really good designer. It's like a good surfer: You watch and it looks easy. And when you try it, it's like, whooah!" You realize how good they are when you realise that you aren't.

"I would say that his work is almost banal," says Renzo di Renzo, editor in chief of *Colors* magazine. "But it's the 'almost' which is crucial." "I like things to look easy," says Fernando.

It's this that he loves in Tibor Kalman, a graphic hero, whose end goal always was to communicate. Design as means, not end. "He wanted things to look trashy and direct and easy to understand, which means there was an incredible refinement behind it." Like hero, like fan. "Fernando doesn't go on about design, design, design," says Telmo. He just does it. With an eye on the words, an eye on the page, so that they don't compete. It's a rare skill in a crowded magazine world where pages scream for attention. When you have to crane your neck to read because the type is overpowering, and you give up from sheer fatigue.

There is a museum catalog, for example, that Fernando shows me, wincing. The typography is all wrong. "It's so mannered," he sighs, and it sounds like the worst insult he could make. "The painting has enough emotion, the typography is unnecessary." And he's right. Not that his pages can't be noisy—see *Tentaciones*—but the volume is under control. So that you will still probably turn the page and pick up the book, and Fernando's work will be done. "I just want people to like it. That's enough."

Not everyone does. Some claim that *Colors* is dull, remote, austere. Fernando wouldn't agree on this (even now that he's left the helm), but he'll take other criticisms, and add his own. Like every time he goes to Madrid in summer and sees his bright yellow and black logo for the PhotoEspaña (PHE) festival

Opposite: Identity and book-jacket design for publishing house Losada, 2002.

Las palabras
JEAN - PAUL SARTRE

Escepticismo y fe animal
GEORGE SANTAYANA

Después de la caída
ARTHUR MILLER
Incidente en Vichy

Días hermosos
FRANZ INNERHOFER

De espaldas a nosotros
MIGUEL BERMEJO

Cielos de espanto
ALDO ZARGANI

Cuentos completos
ROBERTO ARLT

La cuestión humana
FRANÇOIS EMMANUEL

Autobiografía psíquica
HERMANN BROCH

Charlas sobre educación
Pedagogía infantil
ALAIN

El ángel en el tejado
RUSSELL BANKS

La espada dormida
y otros cuentos
MANUEL PEYROU

Curso de lingüística general
FERDINAND DE SAUSSURE

Ensayos completos
KAREN BLIXEN

La Confesión de Agustín
JEAN-FRANÇOIS LYOTARD

La voz de Tianyi
FRANÇOIS CHENG

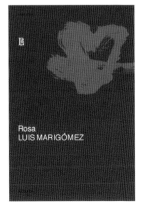

Rosa
LUIS MARIGÓMEZ

Los cuarenta días
del Musa Dagh
FRANZ WERFEL

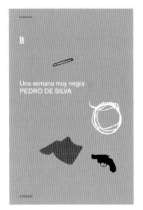

Una semana muy negra
PEDRO DE SILVA

everywhere. He finds its ubiquity frightening, but not only that: He has great expectations, of himself and his colleagues—expectations that are sometimes met, by Marion Deuchars, for instance, whose safe hands are illustrating the 3,000-strong Losada back catalog. Or by Valentín Vallhonrat, who presented a full-bleed, full-on portrait of the then-unknown Alek Wek for a *Matador* cover, which Fernando still talks about with a sigh of contentment, because it was exactly what he had wanted, without knowing. But sometimes the expectations fall short, when people don't understand when to follow his codes and when to break them. (His work ethic, once described as "famously intensive," takes no prisoners.) He wants to go back to the PHE identity and look at it again.

Though it's unlikely he'll have time, now that the Prado is on his client list. It gives him palpitations to think of the vastness of the project, though Prado director Miguel Zugaza is unconcerned. "He understands what it needs." Care, patience, and nurturing. So there's a new bag here, a logo there, a new typography. No hurry, when the Prado has been slumbering for decades. In the hands of a modern traditionalist at ease in his own time and others, its twenty-first century awakening is unlikely to be rude.

Above: New identity for the Museo Nacional del Prado, Madrid, and promotional campaign for the Manet en el Prado *exhibition, both 2003.* **Opposite:** *Promotional campaign for the Titian exhibition at the Museo Nacional del Prado, Madrid, 2003.*

MUSEO NACIONAL
DEL **PRADO**

Tiziano

LORENZO APICELLA was born in Ravello, Italy, and studied architecture at Nottingham University, the Canterbury College of Art, and the Royal College of Art in London. He worked for Skidmore, Owings & Merrill, CZWG, and Imagination before establishing his own London practice, Apicella Associates, in 1989. He brought his team to Pentagram in 1998. He is a member of the Royal Institute of British Architects (RIBA) and a fellow of both the Chartered Society of Designers and the Royal Society of Arts. His work has been widely published and has featured on television and radio. He has served as a visiting critic to numerous schools of architecture and as a validator to the Royal College of Art in London. He is currently an external examiner to both Birmingham and Oxford Brookes universities.

JAMES BIBER studied architecture and biology at Cornell University before establishing his own architectural firm in New York in 1984. In 1991 he was invited to join Pentagram. His team designs a wide range of private and commercial projects, including museums, restaurants, retail, exhibitions, and residences, as well as custom furniture, lighting, and products. In 2000 the team won the commission to design the National Millennium Time Capsule. Currently they are restoring an early modern house by Richard Neutra in Los Angeles and designing a museum for Harley-Davidson in Milwaukee. Biber is a fellow of the American Institute of Architects (AIA), and his work has been recognized with major awards from the AIA, the Municipal Art Society, and the Architectural League of New York. He has taught architecture at Cornell University, Syracuse University and Parsons School of Design.

MICHAEL BIERUT was born in Cleveland, Ohio, and studied graphic design at the University of Cincinnati's College of Design, Architecture, Art and Planning. He worked for ten years at Vignelli Associates before joining Pentagram as a partner in 1990. He has served as national president of the American Institute of Graphic Arts (AIGA), is a member of the Alliance Graphique Internationale (AGI) and in 2003 was named to the Art Directors Club Hall of Fame. Bierut is a senior critic in graphic design at the Yale School of Art and is a coeditor of the anthology series Looking Closer: Critical Writings on Graphic Design and a cofounder of the online journal DesignObserver.com. His commentaries about graphic design in everyday life can be heard on the Public Radio International program Studio 360.

ROBERT BRUNNER studied industrial design at San Jose University and worked at several high-tech companies before founding Lunar Design in 1984. In 1989, he accepted the position of director of industrial design at Apple Computer, where he provided design and direction for all product lines. In 1991 he founded Apple IDg, an independent internal design group. He joined Pentagram as partner in 1996. His work has won twenty-three Industrial Design Excellence Awards from the Industrial Designers Society of America (IDSA) and Business Week magazine, including six "best of category" awards. He holds numerous patents for his work, including both utility and cosmetic patents for the original Macintosh PowerBook design, and his work is included in the permanent collections of the Museum of Modern Art (MoMA) in New York and SF MoMA in San Francisco.

MICHAEL GERICKE received his degree in visual communications from the University of Wisconsin. For the following seven years he worked as a designer and then as an associate at the design firm Communication Arts, participating in a wide range of multidisciplinary projects, including the environmental graphics program for the 1984 New Orleans World's Fair. In 1985 he joined Pentagram's New York office, and was elected partner in 1994. He is a member of the Alliance Graphique Internationale (AGI) and a recipient of Fortune magazine's prestigious Beacon Award for outstanding strategic design. He serves on the advisory board of the Center for Architecture, has been a member of the Executive Committee of the American Institute of Graphic Arts (AIGA), and has taught identity design at the Cooper Union School of Art.

FERNANDO GUTIÉRREZ was born in London to Spanish parents and studied graphic design at the London College of Printing. He started his career at CDT Design in London, becoming an associate in 1991. He relocated to Barcelona, where he worked for Summa, and in 1993 cofounded the partnership Grafica. In 2000 he joined Pentagram as a partner in the London office, and from 2000 to 2003 he was creative director of *Colors* magazine. He is a past president of the European Art Directors Club and a member of the Alliance Graphique Internationale (AGI).

DAVID HILLMAN was educated at the London School of Printing and started as a design assistant at *The Sunday Times Magazine*, eventually becoming editor of its environment section and later redesigning its parent *Sunday Times* newspaper. In 1968 he joined *Nova* magazine as art director and two years later was named deputy editor. In 1975 he set up his own practice and was commissioned to design the new French daily newspaper *Le Matin de Paris*. He became a partner in Pentagram's London office in 1978. He is a fellow of the Chartered Society of Designers and a member of the Alliance Graphique Internationale (AGI). In 1997 he was made a Royal Designer for Industry and in 2001 he was elected international president of AGI. He has edited several books, most recently *Century Makers* (1999) and *Terence Donovan* (2000).

KIT HINRICHS studied at the Art Center College of Design in Pasadena, California, and worked in several New York design offices before starting his own firm, Russell & Hinrichs Design Associates. In 1976 the company moved to San Francisco and formed the national partnership Jonson Pedersen Hinrichs and Shakery. In 1986 the group merged with Pentagram, establishing the San Francisco office. Hinrichs has served as an executive-board member of both Art Center and the American Institute of Graphic Arts (AIGA) and is a member of the Alliance Graphique Internationale (AGI). He is cofounder of *@Issue: The Journal of Business and Design* and is coauthor of four books: *Vegetables* (1985), *Stars & Stripes* (1986), *Typewise* (1991), and *Long May She Wave: A Graphic History of the American Flag* (2001).

ANGUS HYLAND graduated from the Royal College of Art in 1988. He ran his own studio in Soho for ten years before becoming a partner in Pentagram at the age of thirty-four. He has worked with a wide range of clients from both the public and private sectors, including the British Museum, the Crafts Council, Shakespeare's Globe Theatre, Sage, Penguin Books, and Asprey. He is a member of the Alliance Graphique Internationale (AGI). He is the curator of *Picture This*, a British Council exhibition of contemporary illustration, and he has edited (with Roanne Bell) two surveys on the subject, *Pen and Mouse* (2001) and *Hand To Eye* (2003). He is the coauthor (with Emily King) of the publication *c/id*, a critical survey of identity design and branding for the arts.

JOHN MCCONNELL studied at the Maidstone College of Art and began his career in the advertising industry. Between 1963 and 1974 he ran his own graphic design practice where his clients included the influential '60s boutique Biba. In 1967 he cofounded Face Photosetting, and in 1974 he became a partner of Pentagram. In 1985 he received the British Design & Art Direction (D&AD) President's Award for Outstanding Contributions to Design. He is a member of the Royal Mail Stamp Advisory Committee, a past president of D&AD, a member of the Alliance Graphique Internationale (AGI), a fellow of the Chartered Society of Designers, a fellow of the Royal Society of the Arts, and a Royal Designer for Industry. In 2002 he was awarded a special commendation for the Prince Philip Designers Prize.

ABBOTT MILLER was born and raised in Indiana and studied design at the Cooper Union School of Art in New York. In 1989 he founded the multidisciplinary studio Design/Writing/Research in collaboration with Ellen Lupton, and in 1994 he and Lupton were among the first recipients of the Chrysler Award for Innovation in Design. Miller joined Pentagram's New York office as a partner in 1999, and he also maintains a studio in Baltimore. He has been a visiting critic at design schools in the US and abroad, and he teaches a graduate seminar at the Maryland Institute College of Art in Baltimore. He is a member of the Alliance Graphique Internationale (AGI). He is editor of the arts journal *2wice*, and has authored several books on design, including *Design/Writing/Research: Writing on Graphic Design* (1996).

JUSTUS OEHLER was born in Germany, lived in Japan as a child, and attended schools in Greece and France as well as Germany and England. He was educated in visual communication in Munich and began his career in 1985 at Büro Rolf Müller. In 1988 he attended the Central School of Art and Design in London and graduated with a master's degree in graphic design. In 1989 he joined Pentagram and in 1995 was invited to become a partner in the firm. In 2002 he returned to Germany to establish a new Pentagram office in Berlin. He speaks five languages fluently. He has received numerous design awards and is a member of the Alliance Graphique Internationale (AGI).

WOODY PIRTLE was born in Corsicana, Texas, grew up in Shreveport, Louisiana, and studied architecture and fine art at the University of Arkansas. He started his graphic-design career at the Richards Group in Dallas, then ran his own successful practice in Dallas for ten years. In 1988 he relocated to New York and joined Pentagram as a partner. He is a member of the Alliance Graphique Internationale (AGI) and has taught at the School of Visual Arts in New York. He has served on the board of the American Institute of Graphic Arts (AIGA) and in 2003 was awarded the AIGA Medal for distinguished achievement in the field of graphic design.

JOHN RUSHWORTH studied graphic design at Preston College of Art and began his career with Michael Peters Ltd. and Conran Design Group before joining Pentagram in 1983. In 1987 he became Pentagram's first associate, and in 1989, at the age of twenty-nine, he was invited to become a partner, the first to be promoted from within the firm. In 1995 he was elected a member of the Alliance Graphique Internationale (AGI). He serves as an external assessor at Falmouth College of Art and the University of Lancashire.

PAULA SCHER studied at the Tyler School of Art in Philadelphia and began her graphic-design career as an art director at both Atlantic Records and CBS Records in the 1970s. In 1984 she cofounded the firm Koppel & Scher, and in 1991 she joined Pentagram as a partner. She is a member of the Alliance Graphique Internationale (AGI) and the Art Directors Club Hall of Fame. In 2000 she received the Chrysler Award for Innovation in Design, and in 2001 she received the American Institute of Graphic Arts (AIGA) Medal, the profession's highest honor. She holds an honorary doctorate from the Corcoran College of Art and Design, and she has taught at the School of Visual Arts in New York for more than twenty years. In 2002 she published her career monograph *Make It Bigger*.

DJ STOUT is a sixth-generation Texan born in the small West Texas town of Alpine. He received his degree in design communication from Texas Tech University in Lubbock, where he was honored as a distinguished alumnus. Between 1987 and 1999 he was art director of *Texas Monthly*, where he helped to guide the magazine to three National Magazine Awards. Stout joined Pentagram's Austin office as a partner in 2000. In 1998 *American Photo* magazine named him one of its "100 Most Important People in Photography," and in 2004 *I.D. (International Design)* magazine selected Stout for "The *I.D.* Fifty," its annual listing of design innovators. He currently serves on the board of directors of the Austin chapter of the American Institute of Graphic Arts (AIGA).

LISA STRAUSFELD studied art history and computer science at Brown University and earned master's degrees in architecture at Harvard University and in media arts and sciences at the Massachusetts Institute of Technology Media Laboratory, where she served as a research assistant in the Visible Language Workshop under Muriel Cooper. In 1996, with two of her MIT classmates, she cofounded Perspecta, an information architecture software company, and in 1999 she joined Quokka, a digital sports entertainment company, to lead the development of their information visualization products. She has also produced projects from her own studio, InformationArt. In 2002 Strausfeld became a partner in Pentagram's New York office. She teaches interactive design at the Yale University School of Art.

DANIEL WEIL qualified in architecture at the University of Buenos Aires in his native Argentina. He then moved to London to study industrial design at the Royal College of Art, where he received his master's degree in 1981. Following his MA, he cofounded the design partnership Weil and Taylor and designed and manufactured his own products through Parenthesis Ltd. He joined Pentagram as a partner in 1992. He was professor of industrial design, vehicle design and design management (until 1995) at the Royal College of Art, where he is now a senior fellow. His designs can be found in permanent collections around the world, including the Museum of Modern Art (MoMA) in New York and the Victoria & Albert Museum in London.

LOWELL WILLIAMS was educated in fine arts at the University of Houston and trained as a designer with Baxter + Korge in Houston and Saul Bass & Associates in Los Angeles before forming Lowell Williams Design in Houston in 1974. He joined Pentagram as a partner in San Francisco in 1991, and later relocated to his native Texas to establish the firm's Austin office in 1994. Williams is a past president and director of the Art Directors Club of Houston and was a founding member and past president of the Texas Chapter of the American Institute of Graphic Arts (AIGA). He conceived and designed Pentagram's previous monograph, *Pentagram Book Five* (1999).

JANET ABRAMS
is director of the University
of Minnesota Design Institute,
a think tank on public-realm
design. She is also a journalist
and architectural historian.

KURT ANDERSEN
is a bestselling author and
host of *Studio 360*, a weekly
public-radio program about
culture. Previously he was
co-founder and editor of *Spy*
magazine, editor-in-chief of
New York magazine, and *Time*
magazine's architecture and
design critic.

STEPHEN BAYLEY
created the Victoria & Albert
Museum's Boilerhouse Project
and London's Design Museum
that evolved from it. He is
a commentator on design
and popular culture whose books
include *Taste* and *Harley Earl
and the Dream Machine*.

LOUIS BEGLEY
is the author of *Wartime Lies*
and *About Schmidt*, among
other novels. His most recent
novel is *Shipwreck*.

ALAIN DE BOTTON
is a philosopher living in
London. His most recent books
include *How Proust can change
your Life*, *The Consolations
of Philosophy*, and *The Art
of Travel*.

ROBERT DRAPER
is a writer at large for *GQ*
magazine, a former senior
editor at *Texas Monthly*,
and the author of several fiction
and nonfiction books.

OWEN EDWARDS
is the former executive editor
of *American Photographer*,
and is the author of two bestselling design books,
Quintessence and *Elegant
Solutions*. He was the founding
editor of *Parenting* magazine.

ROSE GEORGE
writes features for *The
Independent on Sunday*,
The Guardian, *London Review
of Books*, and *Condé Nast
Traveler*, among others.
She is also features editor
of *Tank* magazine.

PAUL GOLDBERGER
is the architecture critic
of the *New Yorker*, and
the winner of a Pulitzer Prize
in criticism for his writings
in the *New York Times*.

MIKE HICKS
is a designer and writer living
in Austin, Texas. He has
authored several books and
written numerous articles for
Graphis, *Print*, and *Eye*, among
others. His designs are included
in the permanent collection
of the Smithsonian Institution
and he was the founding
president of AIGA Texas.

JOHN HOCKENBERRY
is a design writer and
correspondent for NBC News.
He is the author of *Moving
Violations: War Zones,
Wheelchairs and Declarations
of Independence*, a memoir,
and the novel *A River
Out of Eden*.

KARRIE JACOBS
is an essayist and critic
who writes about architecture
and design for *Metropolis*
and the *New York Times*.
She was the founding editor
of *Dwell* magazine.

EMILY KING
is a writer and curator
with an interest in graphic
design. Recent projects include
editing the book *Designed by
Peter Saville* and the British
Council exhibition *The
Book Corner*. She is designer
editor of *Frieze* magazine.

LANCE KNOBEL
is an independent writer
and strategy adviser.
He has served as an adviser
in the Prime Minister's Strategy
Unit in London and was
formerly editor-in-chief
of *World Link*.

JEREMY MYERSON
is professor of design
studies and co-director
of the Helen Hamlyn
Research Centre at London's
Royal College of Art. He
is the author of a number
of books, including *Rewind;
40 years of Design
and Advertising*.

RICK POYNOR
writes on design and
the visual arts. He is the
founder of *Eye* magazine,
the international review
of graphic communication,
which he edited from 1990–97.
His books include *No More
Rules* and *Obey the Giant:
Life in the Image World*.

BRUCE STERLING
is a science-fiction writer
and journalist from Austin,
Texas. His most recent book
is *Tomorrow Now: Envisioning
the Next Fifty Years*.

DEYAN SUDJIC
established *Blueprint*
magazine, an international
monthly review of
architecture. He also is the
former editor of *Domus*, and
a columnist for the *Observer*.

KURT WEIDEMANN
is a noted author and
type designer. He is a former
professor of the Stuttgart
Academy of Fine Arts and
has published several books
on typography, design,
and language.

LORRAINE WILD
is a graphic designer
in Los Angeles. She teaches
at the California Institute
of the Arts.

SUSAN YELAVICH
is a writer, who specializes
in design and architecture.
Her publications include
Inside Design Now and *Design
for Life*. She is a contributing
editor to various magazines
and in 2003 was awarded
the Rome Prize in Design
from the American Academy
in Rome. The Assistant Director
for Public Programs
at Cooper-Hewitt, National
Design Museum from
1994–2002, Yelavich
co-curated the Museum's
acclaimed 2003 National
Design Triennial.

ACKNOWLEDGMENTS This book focuses on the nineteen designers that comprise the partnership of Pentagram. However we would like to recognize that each of us is supported by both our individual teams of designers and project coordinators, as well as by the administrative staff within each of our offices. We would like to thank all the members of our staff, past and present, whose hard work and dedication has made the projects featured in this book possible.

Susan Yelavich, our guest editor and essayist for *Profile*, understood the nuances of the partnership, our goals for this book, and then captured them with her characteristic grace and intelligence. She skillfully edited essays by twenty different writers so that this book retained their voices even as it spoke to the overarching entity known as Pentagram. Rick Poynor brought his passion for context and history into play for an essay that eloquently conveys the unique business model and social milieu of Pentagram.

Our publisher, Phaidon Press, has proven once again to be an ideal partner. We thank Richard Schlagman, Karen Stein, and Patrick Busse. At Pentagram we owe particular thanks to Steven Bateman, Kurt Koepfle, and Jess Mackta. We'd also like to thank our archivists for their image research: Sally Waterman, Brian Smith, Melinda Lawson, Julie Savasky, and Amy Wimberley. The book is a collective portrait of Pentagram and was led by an editorial board that included Fernando Gutiérrez, Angus Hyland, Abbott Miller, and DJ Stout, all designers with a particular interest in editorial projects. While this group jointly developed the editorial approach of the book and helped steer it to completion, they wisely nominated Fernando Gutiérrez to serve as its designer. We thank Fernando and Susan Jamieson for bringing the project its tactile elegance and visual clarity.

Finally, the role of the *Profile* writers was integral to the conception of this book, and we owe special thanks to an amazing group of diverse authors whose observations about our work made this project an opportunity for reflection as well as celebration.

Pentagram Partners

COMMISSIONED ILLUSTRATORS/PHOTOGRAPHERS Partner group portrait, p. 7: Jens Umbach; Pentagram offices, pp. 9-10, 13-14, 16: Philip Sayer (London), Andrew Bordwin (New York), John Blaustein (San Francisco), Kenny Braun (Austin), Maurice Weiss (Berlin); Partner meeting, pp. 30-34: Philip Sayer; Faber and Faber book covers, p. 47: Charlotte Everest-Philips, Henri Gaudier-Brzeska, Lana Keat, Paul Klee, Andrzej Klimowski, Jannis Kounellis, Wyndham Lewis, Gareth McCarthy, Sam McConnell, Simon Mein, Pierre le Tan, Mark Thomas, Irene von Treskow; New York Jets logo, p. 93: Brett Traylor; Lever Sans type design, p. 97: Jonathan Hoefler, Tobias Frere-Jones; *2wice* covers, p. 135: (top row, left to right) James Wojcik, Robert Polidori, Graham MacIndoe, (second row) Glen Luchford, Martin Schoeller, Andrew Eccles, (bottom row, far right) Christian Witkin; Millennium stamps, p. 177: (top row, left to right) Avril Ramage/Oxford Scientific, Ian McKinnell/Telegraph Colour Library, Bob Miller, Vincent Servanty/Telegraph Colour Library, (second row from top) John Stone, Richard Bryant, Deborah Osborne, Justin Pumfry, (third row) Peter Wood, Photonica/BBC Natural History Unit, Nick Turner, Ken Kirkwood, (fourth row) Andy Earl, Tim Flach/Tony Stone Images, Lorentz Gullachsen, Fluer Olby, (bottom row) Barry Letegan, Telegraph Photo Library, Mike Parsons, David Chalmers; *Long May She Wave* pins, p. 183: Terry Heffernan; @*Issue* cover, p. 184: John Casado; Dreamery packaging, p. 188: Bob Goldstrom, Gary Overacre, Nancy Stahl, Robert Giusti, C.F. Payne, Leland Klanderman, David McCall Johnston, Mark Hess, Kinuko Craft; *Tentaciones* covers pp. 224-225: (left to right) *El País*, Peret/*El País*, Marcus Klinko/*El País*, Jonathan Mannion/*El País*; Compañía de Vinos Telmo Rodríguez labels, p. 226: Sean Mackaoui; Losada book covers, p. 229: Marion Deuchars; Partner portraits, pp. 232-235: Jens Umbach, Mark Van S. (Lisa Strausfeld)

PROJECT PHOTOGRAPHY Peter Aaron/Esto, p. 98; Adam Bartos, pp. 198-201; James Biber, pp. 195-196; Rick Dávila/Museo Nacional del Prado, p. 230; R.A. Hansen, p. 130; Ken Hickey/National Maritime Museum, p. 176; Timothy Hursley, pp. 138-140; Imagination Ltd/Spectrum Communications, p. 104; Peter Mauss/Esto, pp. 74-77, 100, 216, 220-221; Thomas McConnell, pp. 123-125; SAPA, p. 105; Philip Sayer, pp. 88-89; Philip Sayer/Museo Nacional del Prado, p. 231; Dorothea Schwarzhaupt, pp. 192-193; James Shanks, pp. 50, 97-98; Timothy Soar, pp. 103, 107-108; John Stone, p. 144; Nick Turner, pp. 91, 107, 178

LONDON Mely Aguilar, Lorenza Apicella, Steven Bateman, Dan Bernstein, Leigh Brownsword, Teresa Carbajo Garcia, Matthew Clare, Natalie Cronje, Chris Duggan, Jessica Earle, Janice Entwistle, Mark Epstein, Rosie Farr, Fernando Gutiérrez, Zlatko Haban, Charlie Hanson, Ivan Henshell, David Hillman, Angus Hyland, Sharon Hwang, Susan Jamieson, Olivia Jourde, Zach John, Klair Langley, Christine Le Bruchec, Melanie Martinez, Vivien Mason, John McConnell, Kirsty Medhurst, Johanna Mohs, Alison Moore, Lisa Moss, Douglas Nwosu, Deborah Osborne, Claire Parkinson, Bethan Phillips, Lulu Pinney, Jane Plüer, Margaret Pope, Jo Rischmiller, Shellie Robinson, Giovanni Rodolfi, Andrew Ross, John Rushworth, Heather Seekings, Rachel Smith, Dragan Sukljevic, Deborah Taffler, Nick Turner, George Wainwright, Sally Waterman, Daniel Weil, Julia Wyatt

NEW YORK James Anderson, James Biber, Michael Bierut, Don Bilodeau, Marshall Brown, Rion Byrd-Gumus, Tracey Cameron, Michael Clarke, Keith Daigle, Timea Dancs, Gillian de Sousa, Peter Dettmering, Anne Ferril, Colin Forbes, Dinah Fried, Michael Gericke, Stan Goodman, Sunnie Guglielmo, Vivian Hodge, Jeremy Hoffman, Julia Hoffmann, Suzanne Holt, Melissa Jun, Wendy Katcher, Jiae Kim, Kurt Koepfle, John Kudos, Michael Larrieux, Iancu Lascu, Jess Mackta, Joseph Marianek, Su Mathews, Tamara McKenna, Linda Mele-Flynn, Alex Mergold, Abbott Miller, Dolores Phillips, Woody Pirtle, Kerrie Powell, Sharon Rawls, Jennifer Rittner, Kalene Rivers, Paula Scher, Brian Smith, Lisa Strausfeld, Zoe Tasou, Brett Traylor, Lior Vaturi, Andrea Wang, Sarah White, Jack Zerby, Michael Zweck-Bronner

SAN FRANCISCO David Asari, Jackie Astle, Darren Blum, Christy Brand, Bob Brunner, Benjamin Chia, Sean Davin, Tina DeMartini, Rob Duncan, Charlie Dunton, Siegfried Gatty, Mark Goldman, Kit Hinrichs, Belle How, Brian Jacobs, Dana Kurtzman, Tine Latein, Melinda Lawson, Diana Lopez, Julio Martinez, Douglas McDonald, Takayo Muroga, Myrna Newcomb, Charlene O'Grady, Nichol Oyen, Lia Peralta, Rick Peterson, Jon Schleuning, Erik Schmitt, Laura Scott, Jessica Siegel, Victoria Slaker, Holger Struppek, Maria Wenzel, Symon Whitehorn

AUSTIN Wendy Carnegie, Anna Gardner, Kate Iltis, Erin Mayes, Julie Savasky, DJ Stout, Drue Wagner, Lowell Williams, Amy Wimberley

BERLIN Justus Oehler, Josephine Rank, Miriam Tegeler, Uta Tjaden

Phaidon Press Limited
Regent's Wharf
All Saints Street
London N1 9PA

Phaidon Press Inc.
180 Varick Street
New York, NY 10014

www.phaidon.com

First published 2004
© 2004 Phaidon Press Limited

ISBN 0 7148 4377 6

A CIP catalogue record
of this book is available from
the British Library.

All rights reserved.
No part of this publication
may be reproduced, stored
in a retrieval system or
transmitted, in any form
or by any means, electronic,
mechanical, photocopying,
recording or otherwise,
without the written permission
of Phaidon Press Limited.

Designed by Pentagram
Printed in China